TEXTILES IN THE ART INSTITUTE OF CHICAGO

The Art Institute of Chicago

THE ART INSTITUTE OF CHICAGO

Christa C. Mayer Thurman

Edited by Susan F. Rossen, Executive Director of Publications,
and Peter Junker, Assistant Editor, The Art Institute of Chicago.
Production by Katherine Houck Fredrickson, Senior Production Manager,
assisted by Manine Golden, Publications Intern.
Research and editing assisted by Mickey Wright, Research Assistant,
Department of Textiles.
Manuscript prepared by Cris Ligenza, Editorial Secretary.

Designed by Lynn Martin, Chicago.
Typeset in Berkeley by Paul Baker Typography, Inc., Evanston, Illinois.
Fifteen thousand copies were printed on 157 gsm U-Lite
by Dai Nippon Printing Co., Ltd., Tokyo.

All photographs by Nancy K. Finn, Department of Textiles, except:
portrait of Emily Crane Chadbourne, p. 7, Chicago Historical Society;
all other historical photographs, pp. 6, 7, 8: Archives of the Ryerson and
Burnham Libraries, The Art Institute of Chicago. Photo research assisted
by John Smith, Archivist, and Andy Martinez, Archives Technician,
The Art Institute of Chicago.

Hardcover ISBN: 0-8109-3856-1
Softcover ISBN: 0-86559-094-x

Front cover: detail of hanging entitled "The Tamers" (Les Dompteurs)
from the "Grotesques" series, Designed by Jean Baptiste Monnoyer (?) in
the style of Jean Bérain I; woven under Philippe Behagle; France,
Beauvais; late seventeenth/early eighteenth century; wool and silk, slit
and double interlocking tapestry weave (see pp. 60, 61).

Title page: Border designed by Mariano Fortuny y Madrazo; printed and
produced by the Società Anonima Fortuny; Italy, Venice; 1920/30; cotton,
twill weave (pp. 124–25)

Library of Congress Cataloging-in-Publication Data

Art Institute of Chicago.
    Textiles in the Art Institute of Chicago / Christa C. Mayer
Thurman.
        p.   cm.
ISBN 0-8109-3856-1
    1. Textile Fabrics--Illinois--Chicago--Catalogs.   2. Art Institute
of Chicago--Catalogs.   I. Mayer-Thurman, Christa C.   II. Title.
NK8802.C47A783   1992
746'.074'77311--dc20
                                                    92-12418
                                                    CIP

CONTENTS

INTRODUCTION

To many, historic textiles can be intimidating: the techniques are often complicated, the terminology unfamiliar, and the designers and makers mostly anonymous. And yet, textiles are among mankind's earliest and most important art forms. Taking on the challenges posed by textiles, this book seeks to engage the interest of the newcomer and the already initiated alike in this fascinating field. Presented here are eighty-seven examples of European and American textiles — ranging from an early Christian hanging, a Renaissance altarpiece, and eighteenth-century Belgian lace and French silks, to an American quilt and one-of-a-kind art pieces from the second half of the present century — all drawn

Galleries of the Antiquarian Society, 1914

from the collection of The Art Institute of Chicago.

The Art Institute's textile collection began in 1890, when the Antiquarian Society, the museum's oldest and most important support group, gave a number of vestments and tapestries. One of the society's most active and influential members, Martin A. Ryerson,

avidly collected not only paintings and sculptures from all periods, but also decorative arts and textiles. A lumber magnate and the Art Institute's single greatest patron, Ryerson recognized the importance of rare textiles and understood the role they play in the historic, technical, and stylistic evolution of art. Several of Ryerson's remarkable gifts are included here (see pp. 22–23, 32, 34). Some of these he acquired on a visit to Europe in 1894, from which he returned with hundreds of textiles. On another trip, Ryerson was accompanied by Chicago industrialist and museum trustee Edward E. Ayer, who also collected textiles, but gave them to the Industrial Art Division of Chicago's Field Museum of Natural History. In 1906, the Field Museum abolished the section and, following Ryerson's recommendation, transferred Ayer's textiles to the Art Institute, which purchased them the following year. This provided the museum with a fine selection of textiles dating from the thirteenth through the nineteenth centuries (see p. 37). In 1910, again at Ryerson's suggestion, Dr. Paul Schulze, curator of the royal textile collection in Krefeld, Germany, was asked to come to Chicago in order to catalogue the museum's textile holdings.

Another benefactor of immense importance to the history of textile collecting in Chicago was Robert Allerton, a connoisseur and philanthropist of national repute. His association with the Art Institute began in 1915. Among his concerns were practical matters such as the creation of gallery spaces and the museum's first textile facility. In 1927, a section in the Allerton Building was dedicated to containing modest storage facilities, exhibition space, and office quarters.

It was named the Agnes Allerton Wing in honor of Allerton's mother. On his travels, Allerton always kept the museum in mind, returning with textile treasures that he would then give to the Art Institute, either directly or by

Martin A. Ryerson

means of an endowment (see pp. 60, 66, 67, 96, 97). And, at a time when hardly anyone collected contemporary Austrian, French, and German textiles, Allerton laid the foundation for the museum's important twentieth-century yardage collection (see pp. 120, 127, 129).

Ryerson's, Ayer's, and Allerton's understanding of textile collecting was matched by that of several extraordinary Chicago women. Among them was Emily Crane (Mrs. Thomas) Chadbourne. Because she was interested in everything, she collected everything. She had apartments in Paris and in New York, a country place in upstate New York, and a house in Chicago, so space was not an issue. When she gave up her apartments in Paris and New York, truckloads of her belongings arrived at the Art Institute bearing, among other things, costumes, textiles, and sample books from the eighteenth and nineteenth centuries (see pp. 95, 110).

In 1927, several women formed a society to promote the development of the textile arts which became known as the Needlework and Textile Guild of The Art Institute of Chicago. Affiliated at first with the museum's Department of Decorative Arts, the organization, by 1947, had become independent, with facilities located on or near Michigan Avenue. In 1983, the group disbanded because it could no longer meet the rising costs associated with the facilities and a retail operation as well as maintaining a staff, including an artist working on the premises. In its fifty-seven-year association with the Art Institute, the Guild gave forty-seven important pieces to the collection, of which three are featured here (see pp. 18, 76–77, 107).

Another notable donor was Mrs. J. Ogden Armour who, in the 1930s, assembled a collection of shoes. Her purchases, made at auctions, included leather examples dating from the fifteenth through the eighteenth centuries, from archeological sites located near London, as well as the William Beales Redfern Shoe Collection. Redfern was described in his London *Times* obituary in 1923 as "a well-known collector of medieval spurs and gloves of the Elizabethan period." Thus, Chicago inherited overnight, as it were, a little-known but fine historic shoe collection.

In the early days, the textile collection grew mainly through bequests and gifts. While occasional purchases occurred from 1911 on, at a time when the donor list broadened along with the holdings, it was not until a remarkable woman, Belle M. (Mrs. Chauncey B.) Borland, wife of a Chicago stockbroker, dedicated her efforts to this somewhat erratically growing and unbalanced collection, that progress began to be made. Mrs. Borland's interest in textiles was by no means accidental. Her studies at the University of Chicago had included a sojourn in Lyon, for centuries the silk-weaving center of France. There, she pursued her study of Philippe de LaSalle, the famous eighteenth-century designer and technician (see p. 92). Her thesis on him, published as a monograph in 1936, remains a standard reference

Emily Crane Chadbourne

on the subject. Although Mrs. Borland's first gift to the department appears to have been made as early as 1927, her close and long association with the collection's first curator, Mildred Davison, began in the mid-1940s. Through Mrs. Borland's guidance, systematic collecting was

initiated and the collection began to take shape. Ten major pieces she was instrumental in acquiring are illustrated in this volume (pp. 15, 16, 25, 65, 72, 73, 86, 90, 91, 113).

By 1940, it had become evident that the growing textile collection required its own staff. Although the holdings continued to be administered by the

Robert Allerton

Department of Decorative Arts, Mildred Davison, who had joined this department as an assistant in 1923, assumed the task of caring for the textiles. She was named Assistant Curator in Charge of Textiles in 1943. In 1944, she became Associate Curator of Textiles and, in 1960, Curator. One year later, a separate Department of Textiles was founded. Davison retired in early 1968.

I joined the staff in the fall of 1967. Since that time, we have attempted to strengthen the department's holdings in a variety of ways and to expand it in others. Today, the collection contains fifteen thousand pieces and sixty-six thousand swatches. This includes the just-completed transfer to the department of over four thousand textiles of Near and Far Eastern origin. Although, at one point, the collection contained costumes, it was decided during the 1960s and in 1974 to transfer these garments to the Chicago Historical Society. However, in addition to the shoes discussed above, the Art Institute does have precious and early costume accessories such as fans, women's coifs, and waistcoats.

Over the past twenty years, an attempt has been made to create a balanced collection of Western textiles from all periods and in all media. Nonetheless, the holdings are particularly strong in the following areas: Pre-Columbian textiles, sixteenth- and seventeenth-century English embroidered pieces, eighteenth-century European silks, printed fabrics from the eighteenth and nineteenth centuries, nineteenth-century American cover-

Belle M. Borland

lets, Greek Islands needlework, laces from the seventeenth through the nineteenth centuries, English and American examples of the Arts and Crafts movement, twentieth-century

European and American yardage, and one-of-a-kind art pieces.

A number of important acquisitions have been made thanks to the support of the Textile Society of The Art Institute of Chicago, founded in 1978. An integral part of the department, the society boasts today a membership of more than two hundred. It sponsors lectures, tours, and other programs for its members and for the general public, encourages private collecting of textiles, assists with special publications and exhibitions organized and supported by the department, and supplements departmental acquisition funds (see pp. 87, 92, 115, 137).

The department has undergone two major phases of reconstruction, in 1977–78 and in 1986–88, which provided larger and safer storage, spaces for photography and scientific analysis, a conservation laboratory with washing facilities, offices, as well as lecture and study areas. The department's exhibition space was also augmented in 1988 with the addition of the Elizabeth F. Cheney Textile Galleries. The ongoing dedication to the care, exhibition, and research of our holdings is described in depth in *The Department of Textiles at The Art Institute of Chicago* (Chicago, 1989).

Since textiles cannot be on permanent view, due to the dangers of overexposure to the environment, the department undertakes annually three rotating exhibitions that draw on the permanent collections. It has also integrated, again on a rotating basis, textiles with installations of materials in other curatorial departments, in order to provide museum visitors with a broadened understanding and appreciation of the textile medium and to share the range and depth of the museum's permanent collections. Fur-

thermore, the department has inaugurated and hosted many major loan exhibitions accompanied by important catalogues.

Although all of the Art Institute's textiles are now under the jurisdiction

Entrance to the Elizabeth F. Cheney Textile Gallery, 1988

of the Department of Textiles, this book focuses exclusively on Western textiles. A future volume is envisioned to feature the best of the Pre-Columbian and Near and Far Eastern materials, as well as key pieces from other locations around the world. In selecting some of the collection's most important, most typical, and most beautiful examples for this book, an attempt was made to suggest the character of the Art Institute's textile collection, as well as to provide readers with a sense of the evolution of Western textiles. It is hoped that this publication will whet the reader's appetite for a field that is full of splendor and riches.

Christa C. Mayer Thurman
Curator and Conservator
Department of Textiles

TEXTILES IN THE ART INSTITUTE OF CHICAGO

COPTIC TEXTILES

Among the earliest items in the textile collection are those made and used by the Copts, or Christian Egyptians, between the third and twelfth centuries. Because many Coptic textiles—articles of clothing, curtains, or other domestic items—were preserved in arid tombs, a substantial number have survived the centuries in remarkably good condition. A portion of a hanging (pp. 10, 11) is significant for its large size, brilliant, unfaded colors, and imposing composition. Beneath a colonnaded, arched opening stands a warrior garbed in a traditional tunic with clavic bands, the narrow strips that extend from each shoulder, front and back, either to the waist or the full length of the garment. His raised arms may once have held a weapon. The figure's frontality, solemn expression, and animated, sideways glance, as well as the composition's bold lines and strong colors, relate the piece to the often hauntingly realistic portrait icons produced by the Copts. Also reminiscent of these images is the three-dimensional quality of the columns, the warrior's face, and his legs, an effect that is much easier to achieve in painting than it is in weaving.

The hanging is composed of linen warps (see Glossary) and wool and linen wefts (see Glossary), reflecting the materials indigenous to the area. The construction of this piece is elaborate in its use of uncut pile (see Glossary) against a plain weave foundation (see Glossary). This fragment is less common in technique for the Copts, who most frequently used the tapestry weave (see Glossary), as in a wide border (pp. 12–13), once also a portion of a curtain or hanging. In this example, a group of hunters appear in a tightly composed repeat pattern that includes large animal and floral forms.

**Portion of Hanging
with Warrior**
Egypt
Fifth/sixth century

The piece's bright colors contribute to its engaging expression of naive fantasy, created in part by the weaver's whimsical combination of sea, land, and air creatures, drawn from various sources, without regard to scale.

Wide Border
Egypt
Sixth/eighth century

**Fragment
with Nazrid
Coat of Arms**
Spain
Circa 1400

14

EARLY
WESTERN
SILKS

Silk has always been coveted as the
finest and richest of all fibers woven
into cloth. The filament created and
spun into a cocoon by the larva of the
silk moth, silk was exported from
China to Europe from as early as the
third century B.C. During the Middle
Ages and the Renaissance, sericulture,
as the raising of silk worms and the
production of silk is known, flourished
both in Italy and in Spain. Italian silks
were so renowned that they were exported to places as far away as Damas-
cus and Calcutta.

Given the long-established trade in
silk fabrics and other goods between
East and West, it is not surprising how
closely Italian and Spanish silks from
the thirteenth through the fifteenth
centuries resemble Eastern designs. In
fact, the style of textiles woven in the
Islamic south of Spain, or by Moor-
ish weavers in the north, came to be
known as Hispano-Moresque. An
example from around 1400 (p. 14)
features a meandering, undulating
floral pattern combined with prancing
lions and coats of arms carrying an
inscription in Kufic, an early form of
Arabic, that translates to: "Glory to
our Lord the Sultan." The arms are
of the Nazrid Dynasty of Granada.

While guild regulations controlled
all phases of silk manufacture in
Europe, the industry actually remained

Fragment
Italy
Thirteenth/fourteenth
century

in the hands of merchants. They imported raw silk, oversaw the fiber's washing and reeling, negotiated for its dyeing and weaving, and controlled its selling and export. The best customers for silk during this time were the church and the nobility.

Numerous fragments exist that were once part of vestments or secular garb. Some are precisely documented, as in the case of a fragment (p. 15) that was originally part of a mantle belonging to Doña Leonora, daughter-in-law of the Spanish king Ferdinand III of León and Castile (r. 1217–52). Both she and her husband, Don Felipe, were buried in Villacazar de Sirga, near Palencia, wrapped in elaborately embellished garments. The energetic geometric pattern of the mantle fragment incorporates the repeated word "blessing" in Kufic. The fabric was

further enriched with gold thread.

In two fragments of another Spanish textile (pp. 18, 19), an inscription, "I am for pleasure; for pleasure am I/He who beholds me sees joy and delight," plays a major role. The abstract quality of the Kufic script lends itself well to this striking, interlocking design, which can be enjoyed both vertically and horizontally.

Notable for its striking combination of blues and greens is a panel from the thirteenth or fourteenth century (p. 16) with a quatrefoil design, a four-lobed framing device used frequently by medieval sculptors, miniaturists, and ceramic-tile designers. Each quatrefoil enframes a lion standing before a tree and is surrounded by a grid of squares containing dragons, chevrons, and floral patterns. The precision of the design recalls examples of medieval

Fragment
Egypt or Syria, Mamluk
Fourteenth/fifteenth
century

Two Fragments
Spain
Fifteenth century

metalwork, a connection enhanced by the incorporation of gold threads.

Yet, not all European silks came from Spain and Italy. In fact, the survival of fragments produced in Egypt during the reign of the Mamluks (see p. 17), who dominated Egypt and parts of the Near East from about 1250 until the beginning of the sixteenth century, demonstrates the value placed on such exotic material in Renaissance Europe. Mamluk silks such as this example, with its fine geometric design, were sometimes utilized for priestly vestments, the lighter ones as linings, a use that acknowledged the degree to which they were prized. The silk lining was close to the body of the wearer as he performed the acts of the holy sacraments. Sometimes Italian or Spanish silk comprised the garment's outer layer; this would have presented an arresting outward sign of the importance of the rituals and the man enacting them.

Throughout the centuries, the richest and most sumptuous of all weaves has been the velvet weave (see Glossary). In this technique, a second warp thread forms loops that are either cut or left uncut, creating pile (see separate entries in Glossary), the particularly lush texture that makes velvet what it is. Weaving velvet on hand-operated looms required mastery of a highly sophisticated and demanding process in which ground weave (see Glossary), pile (sometimes produced in differing heights), and all additional embellishing, or brocading (see Glossary), with either silver or gold threads, were produced at the same time.

While ateliers created standard compositions that consumers purchased

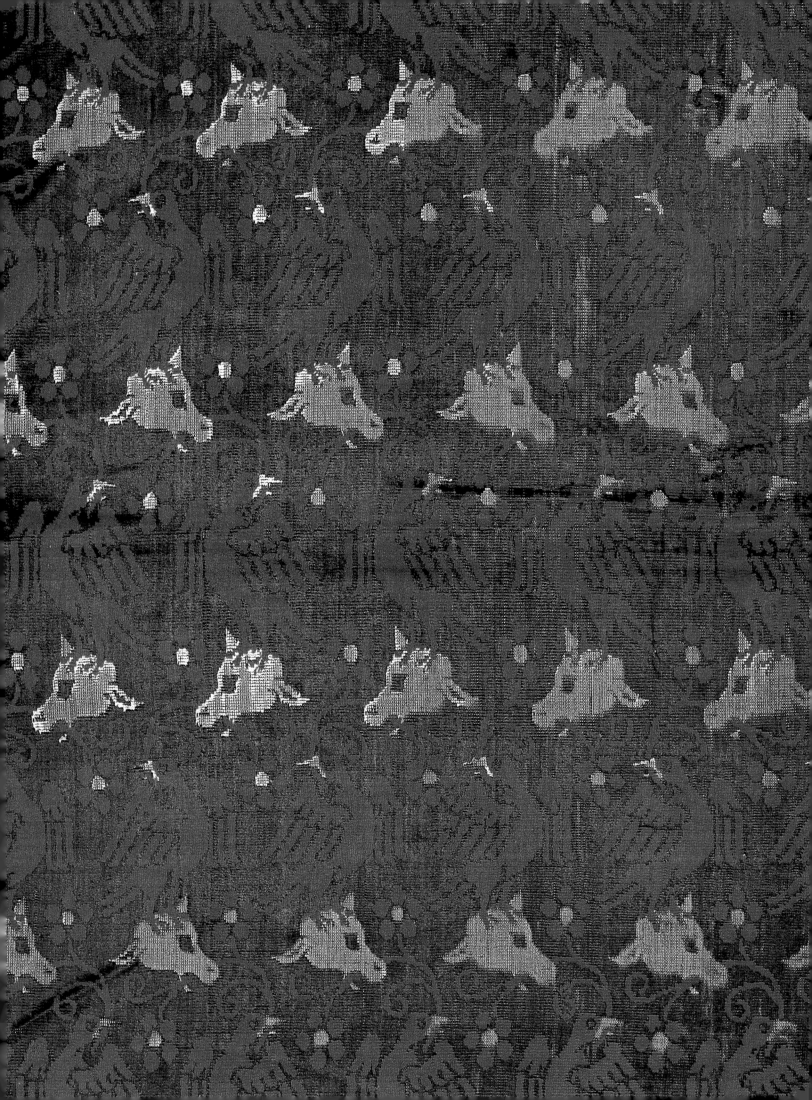

for various uses, they also produced textiles to order. One example of velvet in the collection (p. 20) features a design, perhaps a family crest, with calves' or oxen's heads and eagles linked by floral tendrils. This fragment, from Italy, was once part of a splendid garment worn at only the most special of occasions. It is remarkable not only for the unusually large size of the pattern, but also because the weaver ambitiously incorporated three different colors—blue, red, and white—into the design.

During the Renaissance, Italy led the world in the creation of magnificent velvets, with the cities of Venice, Genoa, Lucca, and Florence becoming world-famous for their production of the material. An altar frontal (p. 21) displays a motif that abounds in Italian velvets of this period: the pomegranate. Its presentation from textile to textile can vary widely in scale and in pattern, from the highly schematic and symmetrical to the meandering and open. Used in liturgical vestments and church decorations, as well as in elaborate secular garments and striking hangings, velvet captivated not only the privileged few who could afford this most costly material, but also painters, graphic artists, and tapestry designers, who depicted velvets in their compositions (see, for example, the woman's clothing in the Swiss tapestry illustrated on page 39).

LATER SILKS

Italian dominance over silk production in Europe continued into the seventeenth century, when the leadership of the industry gradually passed to France. Two Italian silks (pp. 22–23, 24), dating from the sixteenth and early seventeenth centuries, illustrate both the continuation of certain traditions of silk designing and the introduction of new approaches. Designs with such motifs as lions, interlocking tendrils, and floral patterns, arranged in strict symmetry, date far back into the history of silk design. Some of these silks have repeats as large as those of sixteenth-century velvets, but they are designed with a greater freedom and often with motifs repeated in mirror image along a vertical axis. Other silks were, for the first time, designed specifically for clothing, with similar patterns woven on a smaller scale. The pattern of the furnishing silk on pages 22–23 is of a type that could have also been used for dress.

A Spanish example (p. 25), constructed in the satin damask weave

(see Glossary), is strongly heraldic in character. Its boldly conceived pattern incorporates many elements, including the lion of León, the book and shell of Santiago, the castle of Castile (complete with arms holding swords aloft), and a bishop's miter and crozier. The piece is actually a hood that was originally attached to a cope (a ceremonial garment used by clergy or members of royalty during processions), made of identical fabric, now in the Musée Historique des Tissus, Lyon. The hood's gold-and-red color scheme on an off-white ground is enhanced by brocading. Brocading became to weaving what embroidering (see Glossary) is to a finished fabric. Both techniques confine themselves strictly to the patterning areas and do not run the full width of the fabric, or from selvage to selvage, the vertical, warp edges of a textile.

Panel
Italy
Late sixteenth/
early seventeenth
century

23

Fragment
Italy
Sixteenth
century

26

GLORY TO GOD: ALTARPIECES AND CHASUBLES

One of the masterworks of Renaissance art in the United States is an altarpiece (pp. 28, 29) originally acquired for the Cathedral of Burgo de Osma in Spain about 1468 by Pedro de Montoya, Bishop of Osma. This monumental piece, constructed entirely in textile techniques, follows the basic design, iconography, and architecture of carved and painted prototypes. Textiles have often been the result of collaborative relationships between designers (trained as painters), weavers, embroiderers, and sculptors. This is true of the altarpiece. Its upper portion (or retable) represents a triptych with scenes from the life of Christ. The Resurrection and six standing apostles are featured in the lower portion, known as the altar frontal (or antependium). The naturalism of the figurative scenes, the substitution of landscape settings for the more traditional gold background, and the interest in precise description of various textile techniques (see p. 29) all reflect the influence of Flemish art in Spain during the fifteenth century. A remarkable feature of the altarpiece, especially in the retable, is the degree to which the embroiderers were able to create an illusion of depth. The *or nué* technique (see Glossary) was worked over heavily padded areas, producing architectural enframements complete with colonnettes and vaults. The laid work (see Glossary) creates subtle shading to suggest shadows cast by the architectural elements. The rich visual effect of the altarpiece's velvet, silk, gold and silver threads, seed pearls, and handmade spangles, sparkling in flickering candlelight, must have created a compelling atmosphere for contemplation and prayer.

When a priest celebrates Mass, he wears a prescribed ensemble of garments known as vestments. The outermost ceremonial vestment is the chasuble, which can be decorated with orphrey bands. These are usually straight on the chasuble's front and cross or Y-shaped on its back. They served a double purpose, being both liturgical and decorative.

Chasuble Front with Orphrey Cross
Chasuble: Italy, Florence, fifteenth century. Orphrey cross: Bohemia or Germany, first half of fifteenth century

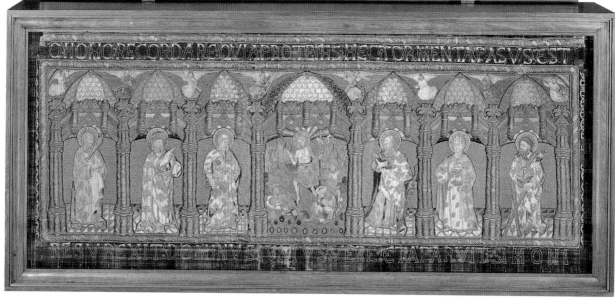

**Retable and
Altar Frontal**
Spain,
Burgo de Osma
Circa 1468

**Altar Frontal
Depicting Scenes from
the Life of Christ**
Spain, Leridà Province
Late sixteenth century

A magnificent, fifteenth-century Florentine velvet, heavily brocaded in gold thread, was used to create an elaborately decorated chasuble (pp. 26, 27). This vestment carries a German or Bohemian orphrey cross, which incorporates Saint George with the dragon (detail, p. 26), and the martyred saints Barbara, Catherine, Sebastian, and Ursula. These figurative scenes recall those depicted on small, ancillary panels (called predelle) of painted altarpieces, as well as in woodcuts and manuscript illuminations

of the period, which indicates that the embroiderer was well versed in the visual arts and trained to follow sketches provided for him.

Like the chasuble, a striking altar frontal (pp. 30, 31), originally intended for the Spanish Cathedral of Seo de Urgel, resembles contemporaneous paintings. Three large roundels, enframed by interlaced bands, or strapwork, feature events from the life of Christ: the Last Supper (detail, p. 30), Christ suffering in the Garden of Gethsemane, and the Entombment. Griffons hold banderoles that display biblical inscriptions in Latin relating to each scene. The smaller roundels in the border illustrate events from the life of the Virgin and of saints John

the Baptist, John the Evangelist, and Jerome. Although the three main roundels are the piece's primary visual focus, the overall composition is unified by swirling lines of embroidered gold and silver threads and by the heavier strapwork, all applied to a velvet foundation. To have created with needle and thread effects as elaborate as those achieved through painting or polychrome wood carving remains the remarkable achievement of the unknown Renaissance embroiderers of this piece.

TAPESTRIES FOR CHURCH AND CASTLE

A universal technique, tapestry weaving reached its most refined and sophisticated expression in Europe from the late Middle Ages through the eighteenth century. Tapestries are based on actual-sized cartoons or drawings that often originated in a painter's studio. Traditionally, tapestry weavers worked mainly with wool, although, in later centuries, they employed linen warps. From the fifteenth century on, silk was often combined with wool to produce finer work and highlights, since silk has a far greater sheen than wool and is a thin-

ner fiber. Tapestries functioned both as decoration and as insulation in castles and churches. They were also used to line streets for ceremonial occasions. A very expensive art form, tapestries came to be closely connected with the ruling classes and the clergy. Centers of tapestry production developed across Europe, although the Flemish and French achieved pre-eminence in the technique, influencing the development of the art elsewhere.

Among the first to bring northern European tapestry weavers to Italy were the Gonzagas, the ruling family of Mantua, for whom the Art Institute's Annunciation scene (pp. 32, 33) was

made. The tapestry is believed to have been designed by Andrea Mantegna, the renowned Renaissance artist who served as the Gonzagas' court painter until his death in 1506. Elegant and refined both in design and technique, the panel illustrates well the close connections that existed between painting and tapestry making. The elaborate furnishings and decorations of the loggia, or porch, in which the Virgin kneels in prayer, the angel Gabriel carrying a banderole with a Latin inscription, the vista of an Umbrian town in the background (detail, p. 33), the

splendid garden laden with flowers
and fruits—all present a feast of visual
delights. The relationship between this
image and painted prototypes is rein-
forced by the inclusion of an imitation
marble frame.

A Flemish tapestry (pp. 34, 35)
shows the Holy Family as interpreted
by an unknown northern European

painter and weaver during the early
sixteenth century. This finely woven
devotional image was used for private
worship, as were the many small votive
paintings of the period that it resembles. And, like them, the tapestry is
charged with symbolism. The chalice
and bunches of grapes held by members of the Holy Family refer to the
Eucharist. A closed book, undoubtedly
the Old Testament, is included beneath

the Madonna's hands; in the background, a knotted rope slung around
a column foreshadows the flagellation
of Christ. The weaver's consummate
skill in imitating pictorial effects is
demonstrated in the globe seen before
Christ, which shows the reflection of
the infant's hand holding grapes and
pointing to the cross above.

TEXTILES FOR DAILY LIFE

Because fine textiles created for either the clergy or nobility were not worn continuously and received care when not in use, they have tended to survive more frequently than less expensive fabrics that served more ordinary purposes, and that were used, washed, and replaced. An example of a relatively humble textile is a German embroidered square showing the Last Supper (p. 37). Made between 1300 and 1310 by nuns in a southern Lower Saxonian convent, the square is the earliest piece of German needlework in the Art Institute's collection. Even the simplest of chapels required furnishings; this panel once formed, along with other squares, part of what was either an altar cloth or hanging. The simplified presentation of the figures — Christ with Saint John sleeping at his left, Judas on the far side of the table, and Saint Peter to the right — facilitates an immediate recognition of the story. This panel lacks the highly embellished appearance achieved through the use of gold and silver threads typical of the more costly and ambitious altar frontals of wealthier churches. Nonetheless, the ensemble of which this panel was part must have impressed with its bold patterns, inspired in part, perhaps, by Hispano-Moresque woven designs, which are used as filling stitches. Known as white or German work (*Opus Teutonicum*), these textiles were made using a technique called pulled thread work

(see Glossary). The composition was embroidered in various stitches employing white, brown, and blue linen with highlights of colored silks in light red, light brown, and green.

Domestic items such as towels, overtowels, or table covers, embellished with designs of dragons or birds, decorated many household interiors, as can be seen in depictions of rooms found in illuminated manuscripts and panel paintings of the late Middle Ages and early Renaissance. An industry to produce domestic ware such as the Art Institute's towel (p. 40) flourished during the fifteenth century in Perugia, Italy. Although the dragon pattern gives the impression of having been embroidered, it was, in fact, woven in blue linen with loosely inserted patterning wefts (see Glossary). The patterned bands appear at both ends of the towel, while the center was woven in a diamond twill weave (see Glossary) in natural linen, a material that can sustain heavy use and regular washing.

A tapestry (pp. 38–39) woven in Basel, Switzerland, at the end of the fifteenth century, features a subject that was particularly popular during the late Middle Ages and early Renaissance, that of love and courtship. Sometimes tapestries of this type were intended as wedding gifts, to be hung in the home as decorations. The young couple's new-found love is symbolized by a doe seated on the woman's lap — a wild creature has become a lap pet. The singing bird between them is symbolic of exchanged promises. The

inclusion of other birds perhaps identifies the scene as part of a hunt, from which the two lovers have separated themselves to spend some time alone together. Inscriptions in Swiss-German convey messages of loyalty: He says, "I love you faithfully," and she replies, "I hope you will never regret it." The figures are set against a rich, densely patterned background of acanthus leaves, flowers, and birds. The style of the couple's attire dates the piece; bound in fur, the woman's dress is made of expensive Italian velvet, which illustrates another use of such fabrics (see p. 21). The tapestry's colors are nearly as vibrant as they were when the piece was woven five hundred years ago.

By the seventeenth century, linen combined with wool was widely employed for curtains, bedcurtains, and bedcoverings. Such fabrics provided thickness and warmth. A panel (p. 41) from Schleswig-Holstein (part of Denmark until 1815) presents a charming design utilizing horizontal, mirror-image repeats. The panel's quaint interpretation of Christ entering Jerusalem was taken from a pattern book that provided motifs for a variety of scenes to be woven or embroidered. The panel's weave structure afforded the additional advantage of creating a reversible fabric, producing a light and dark side simultaneously, both of which could be used.

Hanging Entitled "The Lovers"
Switzerland, Basel
1490/1500

Towel
Italy, Perugia
Fifteenth century

40

Cope
England
Late fifteenth/
early sixteenth
century

THE SPLENDOR OF VESTMENTS

From the Middle Ages to the Reformation, the production of objects, in every medium, for the Roman Catholic Church constituted an immense industry throughout Europe. A major aspect of this activity was the manufacture of textiles intended for use in churches as altar frontals, hangings, and furnishing fabrics, as well as for priestly garments. The owners of such magnificent liturgical vestments, created over the centuries, knew their importance full well and preserved them in church treasuries. It is for this reason that silks and examples of needlework of the medieval period are represented almost entirely by ecclesiastical, rather than by secular pieces.

Among the liturgical garments singled out for embellishment were the chasuble and the cope. The chasuble was the outer vestment worn by the celebrant of the Mass. Originally, it was bell-shaped and all-enveloping, but later it was reduced to a flat, two-sided garment. The cope is a semicircular cloak worn over the chasuble in processions and for special ceremonies.

English needlework was internationally famous from before the medieval period, but was particularly renowned during the thirteenth century, when many examples were acquired by secular rulers and by leading churchmen, including popes. In the papal inventories, and elsewhere, the term *Opus Anglicanum* (English work) was used to describe the embroidered vestments. They were made by professional embroiderers, both men and women, who had served long apprenticeships under the rigidly-controlled guild system that was similarly applied to other craftsmen such as metalworkers, painters, and sculptors.

One of the Art Institute's most treasured textiles is a splendid velvet cope (pp. 42, 43) made in England during

Chasuble Depicting the Baptism of Christ
Italy
Medallion: after fresco by Andrea del Sarto, after 1517.
Chasuble: early seventeenth century

Cope
Spain
Seventeenth
century

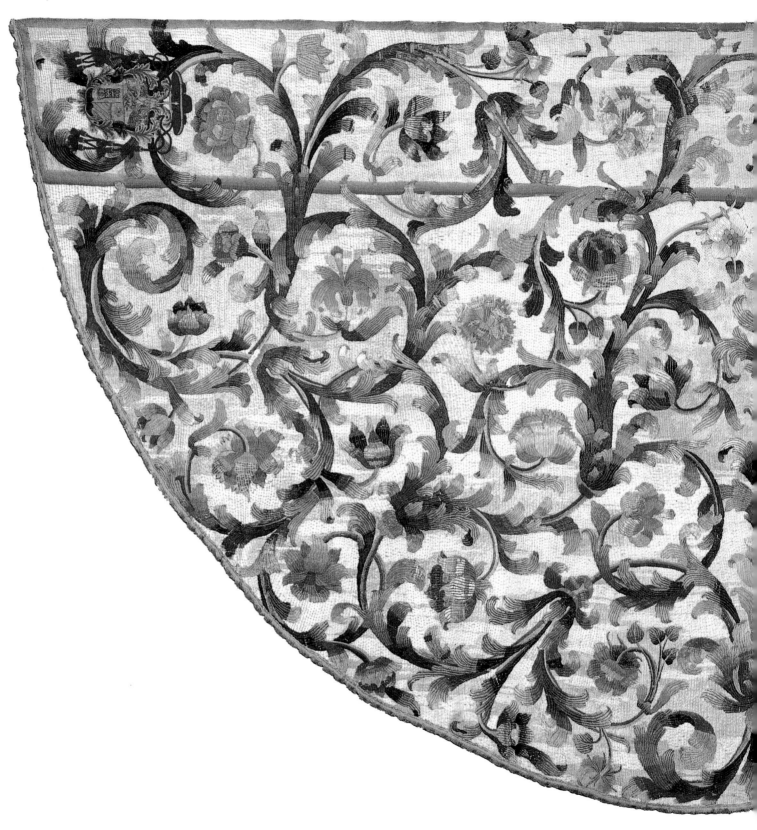

46

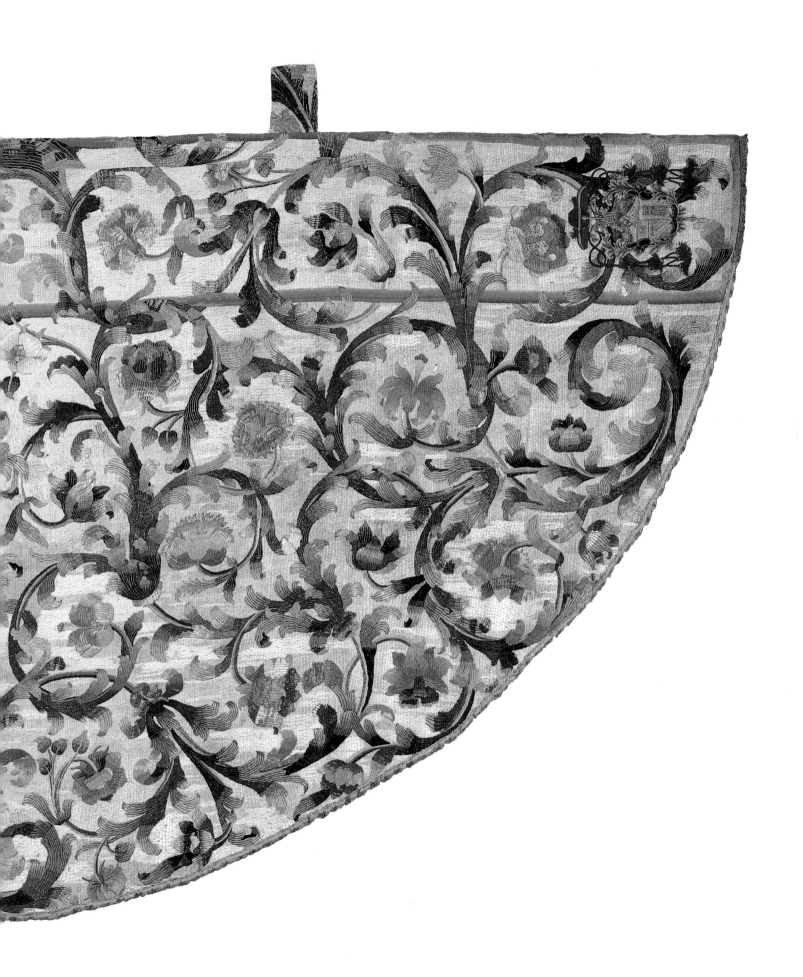

the late fifteenth or early sixteenth century. The orphrey band, hood, and morse (closure) show, respectively, prophets and saints, Saint Paul, and God the Father holding an orb, all rendered with silks and gold threads in closely-worked laid and couched stitches (see separate entries in Glossary). The cope's needlework includes double-headed eagles, thistles, fleurs de lis, and seraphim standing on wheels, all connected by tendrils enlivened by metal spangles. The central image on the back, portraying the Assumption of the Virgin (detail, p. 43), was worked separately and subsequently attached through stitching to the cope. The cope is unusual in that its history is known. It belonged to the Abbey of Whalley until the monastery was dissolved during the reign of Henry VIII (1509–47). It then entered the collection of Sir John Towneley (1473–1541), in whose family it remained until 1922, when it was sold at auction.

Less secular in appearance is an Italian chasuble whose decoration is executed entirely in needlework (pp. 44, 45). It features, on its reverse, an important tondo (circular scene) showing the baptism of Christ (detail, p. 45), based on a fresco painted by the High Renaissance artist Andrea del Sarto in the Chiostro dello Scalzo in Florence and dating from between 1502 and 1517. Floral cornucopia and cartouchelike motifs surrounding the tondo image date from the late sixteenth or early seventeenth century; the tondo portion is somewhat earlier.

A seventeenth-century cope from Spain (pp. 46–47) is notable for its colorful and dramatic floral design. The embroidered pattern has been achieved by couching. In this cope, the floral arabesques invade the traditional orphrey band, which is discreetly defined by a narrow border and the placement at each end of a coat of arms, identifiable only as that of a cardinal due to the inclusion of his tasseled hat.

Another chasuble (pp. 48, 49), from the early to mid-seventeenth century, is mate to an equally glorious cope also in the Art Institute's collection. Both the chasuble and the cope are either Italian or Sicilian in origin, and the floral design is free of any overt religious connotation, although the orphrey band, heavily encrusted with coral beads, carries a cross on the reverse (detail, p. 49). The coral, along with gold threads, forms a dense pattern of cartouches enclosing flowers, birds, and an unknown coat of arms. The birds can be identified as peacocks, symbols of immortality, and doves, symbols of purity and peace. The beads of coral are also symbolic, in that this material was popularly believed to protect against evil. The sections of the chasuble to the left and right encompass a rich array of flowers, skillfully embroidered in multicolored silks and gold threads.

To donate one's wardrobe of the previous year to the church was the eighteenth century's equivalent of today's charitable tax deduction. Thus, many of the Art Institute's vestments were fashioned from fabrics originally intended for secular use and subsequently converted into clerical attire. Such is the case with a chasuble (p. 51) whose dramatic pattern is of a type known as "bizarre," an adjective it rightfully deserves, since its forms and source of inspiration elude clear identification. Once believed to be Italian, such extravagantly patterned silks are of French origin. They draw on a rich variety of design sources, including elements taken from Far Eastern textiles. This example was executed in a satin damask weave in a rich, dark red silk, heavily brocaded with gold thread.

Another cope (pp. 52–53) features a striking pattern comprised of meandering garlands of two kinds of simulated fur — light and dark. The dark fur is further embellished at intervals by silk-ribbon bows. The offbeat motif seems more appropriate to the elegant garment for which it was originally intended than to a sacred vestment.

Chasuble
France
Early eighteenth
century

51

**Cope with
Self-Orphrey Band**
France
Circa 1765

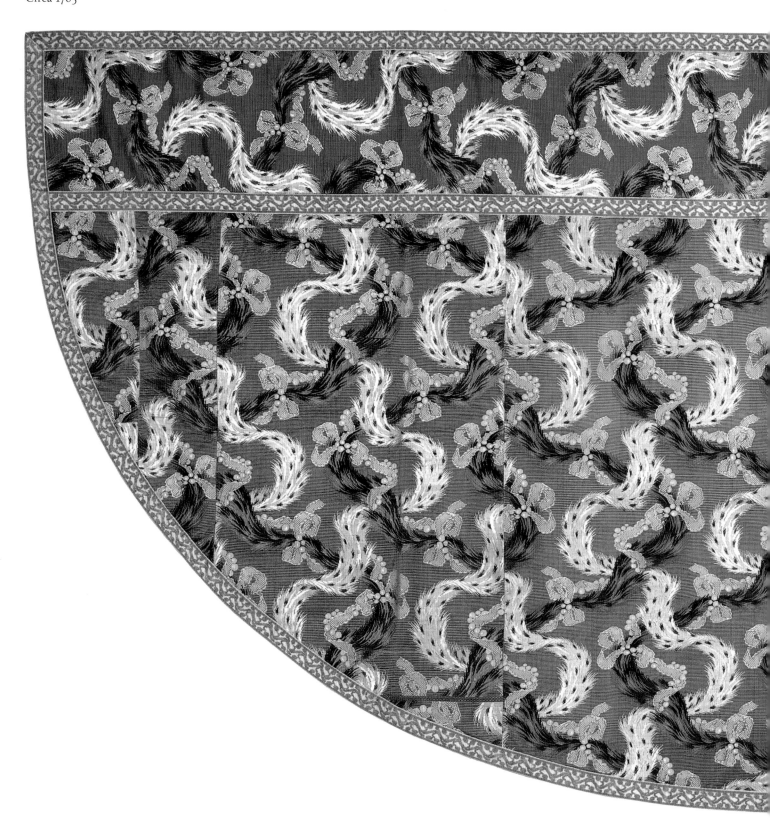

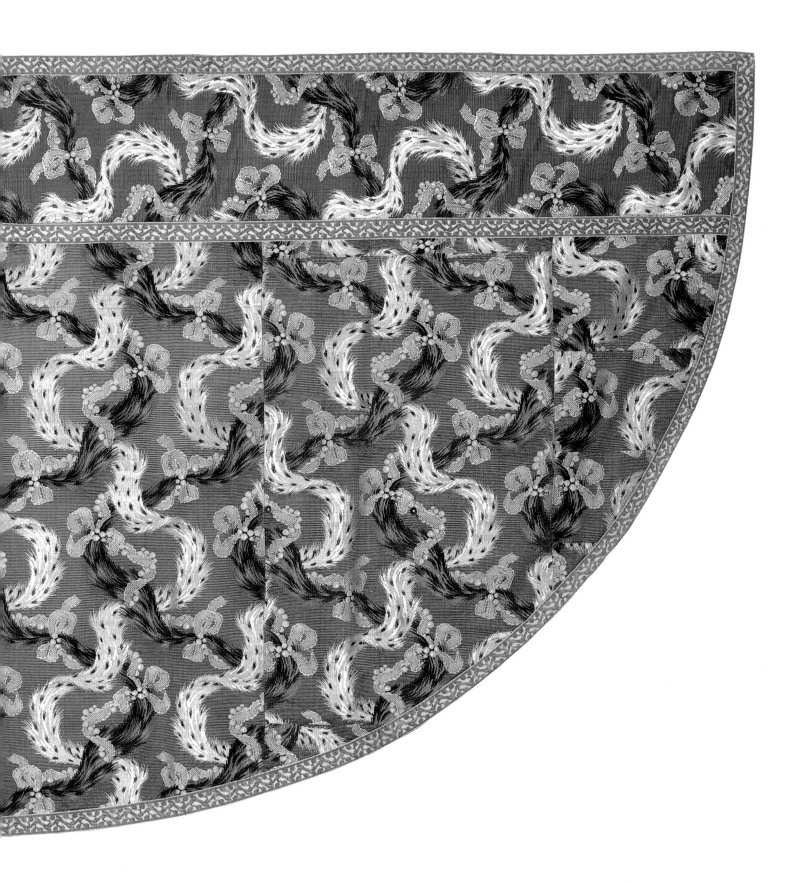

Verdure Tapestry
(detail)
Southern Netherlands
First half of
sixteenth century
(Overall view on
following pages)

THE LARGE, PICTORIAL HANGING

By the early sixteenth century, the center of northern European tapestry manufacture was the Flemish city of Tournai, where a Verdure (pp. 55, 56–57), or "fforest work" tapestry, as the English called it, was produced. The decorative quality of such large-scale tapestries is achieved by a complex composition of swirling branches, leaves, and flowers. Here, birds and animals are to be seen everywhere; and the dense, overall patterning is accented with vibrant colors throughout.

The technique of these large, pictorial tapestries was also utilized to make textiles for other purposes. A mid-seventeenth-century table carpet (pp. 58, 59), executed for the home of a wealthy Dutch burgher, would have been accompanied by matching valances, cushions, and bed curtains. Its function is suggested by its rectangular composition, with a wide border marking the outline of the table over which the carpet was to hang. While its setting and function were secular, its imagery is religious: the central medallion illustrates the Annunciation; and the four medallions in the border present scenes portraying the Nativity, the Annunciation, the Adoration of the Magi, and the Circumcision. The lush and dense pattern of fruits, flowers, and parrots that surrounds the roundels recalls the abundant still-life paintings that were so popular in Holland and Flanders in the seventeenth century. A number of these show how such table carpets provided a rich background for opulent arrangements of food, along with flowers and objects of silver, crystal, pewter, and gilt metal, reflecting the prosperity of the Netherlands in this period.

Given the close connection between tapestry and painting, it is not surprising that the two art forms developed along similar lines. From the sixteenth century on, leading artists such as Raphael, Rubens, Boucher, and Goya provided weavers with cartoons for single tapestries or complete sets. The growing interest in monumental, sweeping compositions, as well as in the portrayal of weighty forms and the illusion of space, led weavers away from the more two-dimensional, overall patterning of earlier tapestries.

While designers and weavers cannot always be identified, some information is known about a tapestry from the French manufactory at Beauvais (pp. 60, 61). The tapestry, one of several from a series called the *Bérain Grotesques*, was woven around the late seventeenth or early eighteenth century under the direction of Philippe Behagle or his son of the same name. Its designer was probably Jean Baptiste Monnoyer, a leading seventeenth-century flower painter, who was clearly influenced by Jean Bérain I, King Louis XIV's chief designer. In fact, Bérain may have provided preliminary sketches for the set, which explains why his name has been connected with the tapestry series from the mid-nineteenth century on. With its playful but symmetrical groupings of canopies or arbors, festooned with garlands of fruit and flowers and harboring classical statues, this tapestry evokes the temporary structures Bérain would have created for the court as sets for royal festivities and performances such as circuses and ballets. Reinforcing this connection are the dancers at the left and right, the lion tamer at the right, and the richly outfitted elephant and rider in the center (detail, front cover), all of which add notes of lightness and frivolity to the scene.

Another French tapestry, woven by Etienne Le Blonde and Jean de la Croix, presents a design by the leading

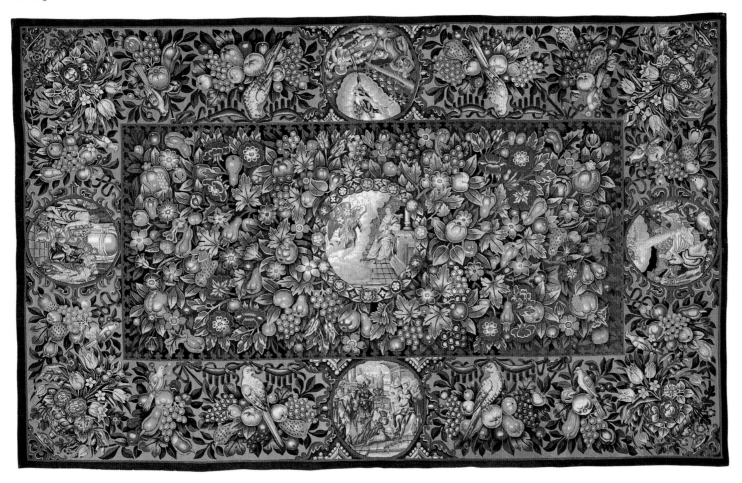

French seventeenth-century artist Charles Le Brun. In 1662, Le Brun's protector, Jean Baptiste Colbert, Louis XIV's minister of finance, purchased for the state a factory that had once belonged to the Gobelins family, a family of cloth dyers. Le Brun became its director. For the next twenty years, the factory produced all types of objects, from bronzes and furniture to lapidary art and tapestries. For the latter, Le

Brun's studio provided cartoons that were followed long after his death.

Among Le Brun's many tapestry designs was a series based on the four seasons, of which the Art Institute owns both "Autumn" (pp. 62, 63) and "Winter." In the "Autumn" scene, two large figures float on a cloud enframed at the top and sides by trees laden with fruit and below by baskets spilling over with harvested fruits and vegetables. In the background can be seen a majestic palace, its abundant walled gardens, and a river heavily trafficked with boats transporting

crops, fish, and other goods. The allegorical figures hold a floral wreath enclosing a scene of a stag hunt. At their feet are additional autumnal symbols: ewers and goblets for wine and hunting equipment. Surrounding the opulent composition is a woven interpretation of a heavily gilded, carved wooden frame that was popular at the time. It incorporates the double-L cipher of Louis XIV.

**Hanging Entitled
"The Tamers"**
Designed by
Jean Baptiste Monnoyer
France, Beauvais
Circa 1700

**Hanging Entitled
"Autumn"**
After cartoon by
Charles LeBrun
France, Paris,
Gobelins Manufactory
Circa 1710

ENGLISH NEEDLEWORK

The English excelled in ecclesiastical needlework during the Middle Ages, as the vestment illustrated on pages 42 and 43 has already demonstrated. During the reign of Queen Elizabeth I (1558–1603), English needlework entered a second period of importance, which was to continue throughout the rule of the Stuarts and after the Restoration. But, in concept and function, needlework changed: It became personal and domestic. English embroiderers, both men and women, worked in royal and affluent households. In addition, itinerant needleworkers could be hired to design and embroider. These needleworkers belonged to the Broderer's Company, a guild founded in 1561, which controlled quality and inspected all pieces. In theory, examples that were judged inferior could be cut up and burned, but the company seems to have had little authority outside London.

A type of needlework associated in particular with Elizabethan England is known as blackwork (see Glossary). The technique involves working black silk thread onto white linen. Sometimes gold or silver threads were also used, as well as spangles. Due to harmful chemical reactions between black iron dye and silk, it is rare to find blackwork in good condition. Two fine specimens of blackwork (see p. 65) entered the collection as pillow covers, or pillow beres, from the collection of the Earl of Abingdon at Rycote House. Recent research has revealed that these pillow covers, along with a panel in the Royal Scottish Museum in Edinburgh, may have been part of a garment similar to that worn by Queen Elizabeth I in an anonymous portrait of 1590 in Jesus College, Oxford. A wealth of stitches defines a lively pattern of leaves and blossoms, interconnected by coiled tendrils, a motif that has been part of the English design vernacular since Celtic times.

A cushion cover (p. 66), one of a pair (the other is in The Metropolitan Museum of Art, New York), carries the initials N. W. and C. W. and the date 1601. Most likely, the covers were meant to celebrate a marriage that took place in 1601. Five of the cover's flowers can be identified as Tudor roses: one in the center (depicted in the traditional rose red and pink) and four variations in the corners. The beautiful, but curious, blossoms alternating with the corner roses are examples of exotic flowers loved by the English at this time. The piece is solidly worked on linen in colorful silks, wool yarns, and linen threads. A border and the original fringe complete the cushion.

Pattern elements that English embroiderers utilized extensively were slip designs (see Glossary) in which individual floral motifs are featured. They could either be presented individually or were combined into considerably larger compositions. The latter is the case for a bedcover (p. 67), dating from around 1620, whose design of floral elements alternating with animals, birds, and insects is arranged in a diagonal repeat. The bedcover's extensive stitch vocabulary, high quality, and superb condition are particularly impressive; yet the needlework was carried out in wool, which is a much thicker yarn and therefore harder to manipulate than silk threads. The animals on the bedcover were copied from pattern books based on bestiaries. In addition to pattern books such as Shorleyker's *Schole-house for the Needle,* published in London in 1624, embroiderers drew upon natural histories, herbals, emblem books, and the Bible for their images.

Sometimes, entire rooms in England were covered with needlework hangings, although Flemish tapestries were generally imported for this purpose. During the second half of the seventeenth century, so-called crewel-embroidered hangings became fashionable. The term refers to needlework composed of wool with a particular

Cushion Cover
England
1601

Bedcover
England
Circa 1620

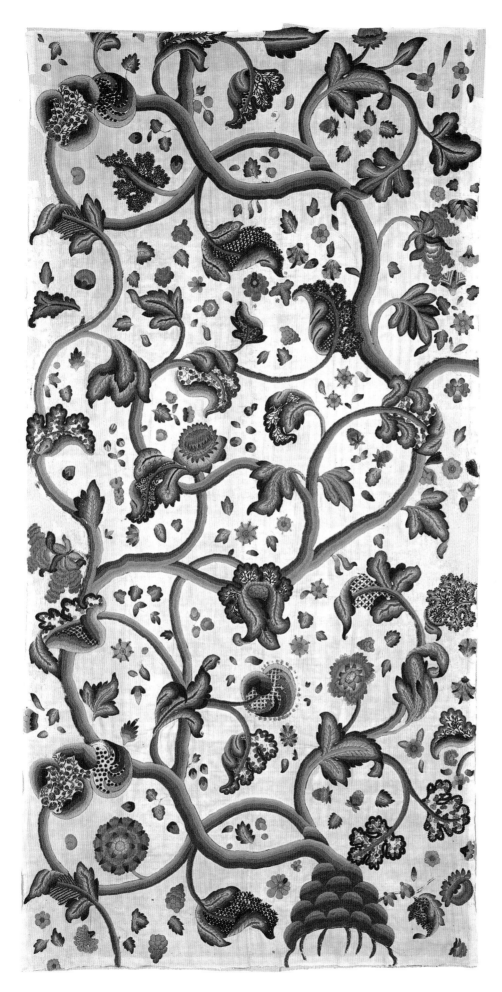

Panel
England
Late seventeenth
century

loose twist. The wool was used in either monochrome or polychrome color schemes and on a supporting fabric woven in a twill or a plain weave in cotton and/or linen. The long panel (pp. 68, 69) was originally part of a bed set, which would have included curtains, valances, pillows, and bed-covers. Designs using wool yarn neces-sitated large-scaled patterns. Here, the bold composition is a curious mixture of elements taken from the large leaf forms found in Netherlandish Verdure tapestries (see pp. 56–57), the flower-ing trees known from Chinese and Indian textiles, as well as typical En-glish characteristics — a varied array of filling stitches (see Glossary).

A magnificent bedcover from about 1720 (pp. 70, 71) is embroidered in yellow and shades of red silk on a cot-ton, plain-woven fabric. The back-ground of the cover is solidly quilted in a swirl of floral blossoms. The com-position is strongly influenced by painted and embroidered Indian and Chinese prototypes. The bedcover relates to a group of equally beautiful examples in museums in Boston, London, Los Angeles, and New York. It has been suggested that all of these bedcovers may have been used atop marriage beds. The pieces in Chicago and London each include a set of pil-low shams.

Bedcover
England
Circa 1720

NEEDLEWORK OBJECTS

By the mid-seventeenth century, professional male embroiderers in England were employed by the court to execute elaborate gold and silver needlework. Professional female embroiderers, on the other hand, specialized in fine needlework on linen. Young girls were introduced to the art at home, where they were trained by itinerant schoolmistresses. High standards were set, and the girls were expected to sew very well. A section of Randle Holme's *Academy of Armory* ([Cheshire], 1688), titled "The School Mistris' Terms of Art for all her ways of Sewing," records a number of techniques and stitches the pupils had to master, such as "raised work, laid work, fingerwork, needlework pearl and purl work."

A sign of individual wealth and prosperity, needlework was used to adorn costume accessories such as caps, bodices, gloves, and stomachers, as well as domestic items such as mirrors, caskets, and embroidered pictures. A partially assembled woman's cap (p. 72), or coif, as it was known in Old English, is skillfully embellished in a variety of stitches in brilliantly colored silks and gold and silver thread. To turn this rectangularly shaped panel into a cap, it was first folded in half and the two top edges joined together for about half their length. The remaining length was tightly gathered to give fullness at the back of the cap. A tape was threaded through the hem of the lower edge of the coif, or through loops attached to it, and pulled tight around the bun at the back of the wearer's head.

It is rare for the name of an embroiderer to be known. In the case of a casket in the collection (p. 73), a piece of paper inserted into one of its secret compartments identifies the maker of the box as Rebecca Stonier Plaisted.

During the time she made the box, she must have married John Plaisted. Two sets of initials, I. (Old English for "J.") P. and R. S., appear with entwined hearts on a back panel. The finishing date of 1668 is rendered in seed pearls on the two front doors of the casket. Two Old Testament stories are depicted on the object: The doors show the Queen of Sheba before Solomon; the top, side, and back panels contain scenes from the story of Abraham and Isaac. The box is further embellished with images of wild and fantastic beasts—a lion, a unicorn, a stag, and a leopard—surrounded by a myriad of flowers, insects, and small animals. A gifted needleworker, Rebecca Plaisted employed an elaborate stitch vocabulary. As a foundation fabric, she used silk woven in satin weave (see

**Unassembled
Woman's Coif**
England
Circa 1600

**Casket Depicting
Scenes from the
Old Testament**
England, 1668

Glossary), which she would have
bought from a London merchant in
the shapes of the various panels and
their patterns drawn out on it in ink.
She would have decided which techniques to use in working the panels.
Large sections of the figurative scenes
are executed in stumpwork, or high
relief; bits of mica, seed pearls, and
coral beads complete the composition.
The finished panels would have been
returned to the merchant to be mount-
ed on a wooden casket fitted out to a
standard pattern to carry writing im-
plements, toilet articles, and jewelry.

As mirror glass was very expensive,
small pieces of glass were normally
inserted into wide frames that could
be embellished in a variety of ways.
Images of kings and queens, perhaps
those of King Charles II and his wife,
Catherine of Braganza, appear twice in
the embroidered frame of a fine seventeenth-century mirror (pp. 74, 75).
They are portrayed in royal garb on
both sides of the mirror and in portrait
busts at its top and bottom. While
secular and mythical subjects are popular in needlework of this period, religious references are still common, as
is the case with this mirror. Seated Old
Testament figures, including Judith
(upper left) and Yael (lower right), are
placed in the corners of the mirror.

Mirror
England
Circa 1665

Panel from Settee
England or France
Mid-eighteenth century

Flowers, birds, and fierce-looking dragons fill the interstices. The preciousness of the Art Institute's mirror is underscored not only by the fine needlework but also by the outer frame, which is made entirely of tortoiseshell.

This luxury item was intended for a young girl's room and may have hung above an embroidered box on her dressing table.

Embroidered fabrics were also used to cover furniture. A shaped panel (pp. 76–77) is the larger of two required to cover a settee (a seat large enough for at least two individuals,

with back and arm sections). The companion piece is in the Abegg Foundation Collection, in Riggisberg, near Berne, Switzerland. The panel's chinoiserie motifs, including pagodas and temples hung with bells, reflect the European preoccupation in the eighteenth century with the Far East. Although it is possible that the fabric is French, the treatment of the small mountains, or hillocks, in the foreground is typical of English needlework of this period. The scene is worked solidly in tent stitches (see Glossary) in brilliantly colored silk threads and woolen yarns.

THE MAGIC OF LACE

There are two broad categories of lace: needle and bobbin (see Glossary). The two groups divide, in turn, into endless types, often carrying Italian or French names, such as *Point de Venise* and *Point d'Alençon*, which reflect the cities and towns that became famous for lace of a certain technique. But as lace makers traveled and worked afield, the techniques and patterns spread, and the nomenclature can be misleading. Thus Valenciennes, Mechlin, and Lille laces were all made beyond the towns that gave them their names.

The earliest examples of needle lace, which probably originated in Italy, retain a balanced, gridlike pattern shaped by the techniques of cut and drawn work (see separate entries in Glossary) from which they developed. A charming French cover (pp. 80–81), dated about 1620/30, comprises

twenty-four squares of white needlework elaborated with cut and drawn work, alternating with twenty-four others of lacis (see Glossary). Each of the individual squares features a unique motif—trees, figures, and animals—taken from bestiaries and pattern books. The individual squares were joined, and then the whole composition was edged with bobbin lace.

A cutwork collar (pp. 78, 79) is filled with large needle lace motifs that anticipate the free needle lace technique. This was made on a parchment pattern rather than on a cut fabric ground. Employing linen thread and buttonhole stitches (see Glossary), the lace maker constructed a lively pattern of figures and animals. Initially conceived as a wide border, this piece was altered at some point and made into a collar.

Bobbin lace also developed in Italy, although it was to be perfected in northern Europe, notably in Flanders.

Its forerunners were the braids made in the passementerie, or ornamental trimming industries of Venice and Milan; like the braids, the early bobbin laces were heavy, plaited trimmings, often made of silk and gold or silver threads, that were laid flat on the surface of clothes and furnishings. Before the end of the sixteenth century, more complex techniques were employed and an increasing number of threads were needed, each wound on a bobbin of wood, bone, or ivory. These were sometimes embellished with brief sayings or the initials of the lace maker.

Bobbin lace is made by attaching paired bobbins, wound with linen threads, to a pillow on top of a piece of parchment on which a pattern has been pricked for the lace maker to follow. To create complex patterns and motifs, sometimes hundreds of bob-

Border Made into a Collar
Italy
Late sixteenth/
early seventeenth
century

Cover
France
1620/30

bins are used at once. In a second form of bobbin lace, individual motifs are made and put together with such skill that only an expert can tell that they have been joined. This is called part lace.

A superb example of part lace is a border in two sections (pp. 82, 83) which includes the inscriptions VIVE LE ROI ("Long live the King"), CAROLUS REX, C B BARONET, and C 1661 B. The type of lace is English, from Devonshire in South Dorset. Recent research has connected this border with a baronet, Sir Copleston Bampfield of Poltimore, in Devon. A strong royalist, he must have been pleased by the restoration to the throne of Charles II in 1660, to which the border's inscriptions probably refer. It is thought that Bampfield received a royal favor in thanks for his support. To celebrate this momentous occasion, he may have commissioned this very special piece of lace for himself.

Lace has enjoyed a multitude of uses, embellishing both liturgical and domestic objects. It has also played a major role in the history of western fashion, adorning the apparel of men as well as women. Lace lappets and cap crowns, cravat ends and veils were made for those who could afford them. A cravat end (p. 84), once belonging to a set of two, was part of a neck piece made for King Louis XIV of France. Created shortly before his death in 1715, the rectangular piece is a fine example of Brussels lace (see Glossary). On the cravat end, the king's double-L's form his monogram and are seen below trophies and a rooster, all

of which symbolize royalty. The image
is surmounted by a baldachin supported by trumpeting angels. To the
right and left appear armed female war-
riors and, in the upper corners, the
Maltese cross and the sun (which

refers to the "Sun King"), all presented
in an elegant and skillful manner.

Though a little lace was still worn
by men during the nineteenth century,
it was by then in greater demand for
the elaborate dresses worn by women,
as well as for shawls, veils, and other
accessories. A particularly spectacular
veil from Belgium (p. 85) was made

for a member of the Russian imperial family, since it carries the family's coat of arms. Constructed in needle lace of a type known as *Point de Gaze* (see Glossary), it would have been attached to a headdress and draped loosely over the wearer's shoulders. By the time this magnificent piece was created, most lace was being produced by machine. Today, the tradition of handmade lace continues, but glorious examples such as this one are no longer made. However, the techniques have been taken up and revitalized within the fiber art movement (see Luba Krejci's *Morpheus*, p. 138).

Cravat End
Belgium, Brussels
1700/15

Veil
Belgium
Late nineteenth
century

SILKS FROM FRANCE AND ENGLAND

In its aspiration to become the fashion center of Europe, France developed a thriving silk industry. Under the direction of King Louis XIV's minister Jean Baptiste Colbert, controls were exerted on the silk trade: Laws were established to regulate quality and price; embargoes were placed on the importation of foreign-made silk; and sumptuary laws were enacted to regulate consumption of silk products. The city of Lyon, where Italian silks had been traded and silks produced since the sixteenth century, became the country's silk capital. In 1660, more than three thousand weavers were active in the city; by the time of the French Revolution, the number of craftsmen employed in the industry was twenty thousand. The French obsession with high fashion and interior decoration sparked the production of bolt upon bolt of fine silks. Designs changed annually and reigning colors altered over the years. At the beginning of the eighteenth century, weavers employed rich colors and incorporated gold and silver threads to achieve sparkle and brilliance.

A striking silk (p. 86) would once have been part of a splendid garment. The incongruous scale of the elements of this pattern, in which oversized fruit and floral shapes are interspersed with minute buildings, is at once witty and reminiscent of pastoral scenes depicted in paintings and prints of the period.

Panel
France, Lyon
Circa 1735

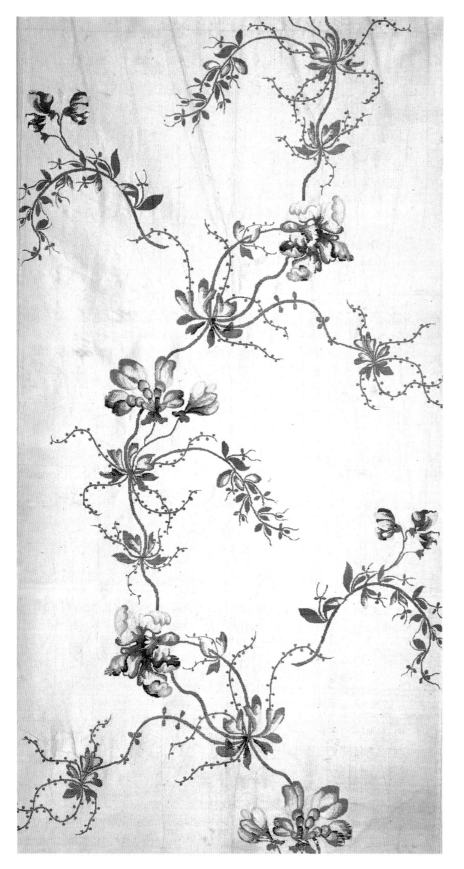

Another inventive design that challenges every law of perspective and scale is found on a French silk composed in fresh, vibrant colors and heavily decorated with silver and gold (p. 87). Within a dense and elaborate pattern of leaves and roots appear clumps of strawberries and violets growing around rocks surmounted by small trees. The repeats are interchanged as the pattern develops into yards and yards of fabric: What appears to the left in one part of the composition appears to the right in the next repeat. Using such dynamic concepts, the designers of silks achieved a sense of rhythm and a fluidity unknown in previous centuries. Like the example on page 86, this silk would have been tailored into a fancy ball gown.

The religious persecutions of the seventeenth century forced hundreds of thousands of French Protestants (Huguenots) to flee France. Many eventually settled in England, where they were instrumental in establishing a silk industry that rivaled the one in France. Huguenot weavers established themselves in a part of London known as Spitalfields, which became the silk-weaving center of England. A textile produced in Spitalfields (p. 88) is possibly the work of Anna Maria Garthwaite, one of England's most outstanding textile designers. "Flowered" silks, as Spitalfields designs became known, can be characterized as using an off-white background onto which brilliantly colored flowers are brocaded, giving the fabric the feeling of

Panel
Designed by
Anna Maria Garthwaite(?)
England, London
Spitalfields, 1741/42

lightness and elegance that is so typical of the Rococo.

French silks woven at Lyon continued to dominate the market; in the later years of the Ancien Régime, some of the most spectacular silks ever woven were produced by important weavers such as Claude Camille Pierre Pernon, Philippe de LaSalle, and Jean Démosthène Dugourc. Pernon served King Louis XVI as principal furnisher of designs to the royal furniture treasury (*Garde meuble*) from 1785 to 1790. In this capacity, he saw to it that LaSalle, his partner, received important commissions. Their business expanded to include materials for furnishings, in addition to fabrics for apparel. Eventually, orders for woven silk were received from such far-flung places as the courts of Russia and Spain. Trained as a painter by François Boucher, among others, LaSalle presented his textile designs not only with visual sophistication but also with an extensive knowledge of weaving techniques. A splendid pattern (p. 92) was commissioned from him about 1775 to decorate the walls of the Russian Empress Catherine II's summer palace at Tsarskoe Selo. With its basket of flowers hanging from a wreath, and its two doves, all set against a dark, rich red ground, this panel is a prime example of LaSalle's appealing designs in the Louis XVI style. Like other designers of furniture, ceramics, and metalwork of this period, LaSalle moved his designs away from the light, freely handled character of the Rococo toward greater centrality and weight. In keeping with this growing preference for simpler, more understated forms, he abhorred heavily brocaded fabrics and refused to incorporate gold and silver threads into his woven yardage.

Pernon's own hand as designer and producer is seen in a magnificent velvet panel (p. 89) intended for the "Velvet Room" at the Casita del Principe in the Pardo Palace near Madrid, Spain. Dating from 1788, the panel is a masterful example of the challenging and difficult chiné technique (see Glossary). Unlike LaSalle, whose compositions feature large design units, Pernon introduced a pattern of repeated, smaller-scale motifs contained within a meandering rhythm.

Closer to LaSalle's style is the work of Dugourc, who was trained as an architect. Educated in Italy for a time, Dugourc was familiar with the antique motifs that Raphael had revived in his fresco decorations for the Loggia at the Vatican. In fact, the French designer titled a group of textile patterns *Vatican Verdures*. "The Pheasants" (p. 90) is part of this series. It was designed as a wall covering for the Casita del Labrador, near Madrid. The elaborate composition encompasses a lavish, symmetrical interplay of birds, baskets, strings of pearls, garlands, and ribbons — all realized with the excellence of workmanship that made French silks so desirable.

The French Revolution struck a lethal blow to the social and economic structures that had encouraged and

**Panel Entitled
"The Pheasants"**
Designed by
Jean Démosthène
Dugourc
France, Lyon
After 1799

sustained the French silk industry, curtailing production drastically and plunging many of its leading figures, including LaSalle, into ruin. But activity did not cease entirely. The Directoire style, so named because it reached its apogee during the short period of the Directorate (1794–99), was appropriately straightforward and austere. Comparison of a panel (p. 91), made by an unknown designer and weaver around 1790, with Dugourc's "Pheasants" illustrates well the Directoire style's bold simplification of the preceding Louis XVI manner. This design, in white on a dark-red ground, would have been arranged, panel next to panel, along the walls of a room, providing a striking backdrop to elegant, attenuated furniture inspired by ancient prototypes and sparingly embellished with Neoclassical motifs.

With Napoleon's ascent to power and his subsequent support, the French decorative arts, seen as an essential part of France's sense of cultural leadership, were reinvigorated in the early years of the nineteenth century. The weaving industry was revolutionized during these years by a number of developments, including the Jacquard attachment, which requires only one operator and is capable of creating complex patterns. Refined by Joseph Marie Jacquard and patented by him in 1805, this complex mechanism is often looked upon as the first computer, since it utilizes punched cards, which function like early computer cards, to create the design. The passage of needles through holes in the cards enabled individual warp threads to be lifted in the weaving of complex patterns. It required great skill to convert the mise-en-carte (the working design on graph paper) onto the punched cards, one of which was needed for each color on each line of the design.

Panel
France, Lyon
Circa 1790

Panel
Designed by
Philippe de LaSalle
France, Lyon
Circa 1775

The weaver used foot pedals to activate the mechanism. But, as with all of the applied arts, increased mechanization also led to slipping standards, inferior training and workmanship, and a paucity of visual ideas.

Throughout the century, a number of styles were revived in quick succession, as designers attempted to reinterpret them with the new technology. The patterns issued by the Lyon firm of Mathevon et Bouvard, among others, are reminiscent of such revival designs, but the quality of weaving and coloration was greatly improved and exhibit once again the superb craftsmanship for which Lyon had been justly celebrated in previous centuries. In pristine condition is a length designed as furnishing fabric and dating sometime between 1860 and 1880 (p. 93), which was preserved for the firm's archive. Its symmetry is softened by an elaborate floral pattern that evokes the lush designs of the late Baroque period.

Panel
Produced by
Mathevon et Bouvard
France, Lyon
1860/80

THE PRINTED CLOTH

Embellishing a plain woven piece of fabric with a design independent from elaborate and time-consuming loom operations has been achieved throughout the ages, in all cultures, and by such methods as tie-dying, ikat, batik, and block printing (see Glossary). The development of textile printing in Europe was slow; early textiles were sometimes colored with oil stains, but these could not be washed. The formation of the English East India Company in 1600 and its counterpart in Holland two years later sparked the influx into the West of painted and printed Indian cotton textiles. Their popularity was such that their importation threatened the wool and silk industries; in England, for example, sumptuary laws were established to limit their use and to prevent the production of local copies. Printing on linen and fustian (see Glossary), however, was allowed, and, by the third quarter of the eighteenth century, printed cotton textiles were also being produced widely, notably in France and England.

A pattern known as "The Flowering Cornucopia" (*La Corne fleurie*; p. 97)

was produced by woodblock printing some time after 1789. It illustrates the capacity of this technique to achieve several colors, although this required a separate block for each color, as well as several to make up the complete design. Here, a vibrant palette is set against a solidly worked, dotted background, or picotage (see Glossary). The striking design of flowers, ribbons, and pearls recalls earlier woven French silks. Textiles such as this one could be used both as a furnishing fabric or for clothing.

Since printing with wooden blocks was laborious, the invention of copper plate printing in 1752 by Francis Nixon at the Drumcondra Printworks near Dublin was of tremendous import. The metal plates could be larger than the heavy wooden blocks, thus making larger repeats possible. In addition, they could be much more finely engraved. The method's major drawback was that, like woodblock printing, it permitted working with only one color at a time. Multiple colors were either added by brush or by additional woodblocks.

French and English printed fabrics were commonly decorated with figural scenes drawn from mythology and history, both ancient and modern, as well as from daily life. An En-

glish panel, "A Visit to Camp" (p. 95), features military scenes inspired by the satiric engravings of Henry Bunbury. An inscription on a drum links this scene with the troops of King George III.

Copper plate printing reached England via Ireland and then found its way to France where, at Jouy-en-Josas, one of the country's most important printing centers was established by Christophe Philippe Oberkampf in 1760. Jean Baptiste Huet, trained as a painter, was chief designer at the Jouy-en-Josas manufactory for twenty-eight years (1782–1811). His chinoiserie scene (p. 96) presents a theme that was of great fascination to Europeans, particularly during the eighteenth century. Entire rooms in palaces and hotels were decorated with furniture, porcelain, metal and lacquerwork, and fabrics, all conceived as whimsical, highly westernized versions of Far Eastern forms, designs, and motifs. Many a European garden encompassed a latticed teahouse or pagoda not unlike those pictured here. Panels such as this would have been used as cover-

Panel
Designed by
Jean Baptiste Huet
France, Nantes
Circa 1786

**Panel Entitled
"The Flowering Cornucopia"**
France, Beautrian, Bordeaux
After 1789

Panel Entitled
"The Merchant of Love"
Designed by
Louis Hippolyte LeBas
France, Jouy-en-Josas
1815/17

ing material for chairs and sofas as well as to cover vast expanses of walls.

Engraved metal roller printing was first used in England, where it was invented in 1783 by the Scotsman Thomas Bell. By the turn of the century, Jouy-en-Josas was utilizing this technology to the fullest. Chief among the advantages of the engraved roller over earlier printing techniques were its speed and its capacity to achieve a greater number of repeat patterns on a smaller scale than had been attempted with copper plate printing. Since the roller could only print one color at a time, additional rollers were used for additional colors. Designs such as "The Merchant of Love" (*La Marchande d'Amour;* p. 98) could be produced in various single colors. This panel, printed at Jouy-en-Josas in 1815/17, combines scenes based on the compositions of French Neoclassical artists who were, in turn, influenced by Roman frescoes and the decorative arts, such as precious cameos, that were rediscovered in the eighteenth century. The source for the most elaborately framed scene is a celebrated work by the French painter Pierre Paul Prud'hon.

An English roller printed fabric (p. 99), created at Lancaster Prints, was intended to be cut and employed as borders for quilts or for furniture coverings. By the mid-nineteenth century, when this panel was made, printers had replaced the old vegetable dyes with ones made from analine or coal-tar dyes, which permitted a whole new color palette. The pattern created by the repeated butterflies is intensified by the use of brilliant colors against a dark background.

Panel
Produced by
Lancaster Prints
England, 1856

REVIVAL AND REFORM MOVEMENTS

The single most powerful influence on the applied arts in Europe and America during the second half of the nineteenth century, the British Arts and Crafts movement developed in response to what many saw as the negative results of the Industrial Revolution. Commercialization, division of labor, and mass-production had precipitated a lowering of standards and of working conditions. The apparent victory of technology over hand processes meant not only the disappearance of fine craftsmanship and inventive design but also signalled the alienation of artisans from their products and the lessening of their position.

These and other tensions, including labor issues and intense competition for new markets, resulted in a system that left little time or energy for the creation of original styles or for skilled workmanship. For much of the century, designers looked to past styles for inspiration, creating a quick succession of revivals emulating classical art, the high Gothic, and Renaissance art. While the revivals produced significant achievements, there was growing objection to these trends. One of the strongest voices of opposition was critic John Ruskin, who became convinced that much about the Industrial Revolution could be counteracted by reintegrating the role of designer and maker, re-establishing the primacy of the handcrafted over the mechanically produced, and reinvesting the crafts with the status of fine art.

These aims were also supported by the influential William Morris — a poet, writer, and political theorist, as well as a gifted artist and designer. For Morris and his devoted followers, the Arts and Crafts movement they founded in the late 1880s became part of the search for a new social order.

Revering the Middle Ages as an ideal time for community and craft, they set up organizations inspired by medieval guilds to train artist-craftsmen and maintain high standards. Many of them moved their workshops out of London to rural settings where the effects of the Industrial Revolution were not yet so pervasive.

Some reactions to the Industrial Revolution were pointedly less political than Morris's. The historian Walter Pater, the artist James McNeil Whistler, and the writer Oscar Wilde became leaders of the Aesthetic movement, which sought to emancipate art from any social or utilitarian function by stressing the supremacy of the aesthetic experience. Like his friend Whistler, the architect and designer Edwin William Godwin became passionately interested in Japanese art, admiring its bold designs and clarity of conception. During the 1850s and '60s, he furnished his home entirely in the Japanese style. He also collected Japanese prints and books. The highly original pattern of a silk panel (pp. 100–101) was stimulated by the forms of Japanese crests and shields. Manufactured by the British firm of Warner & Sons, it is one of the few surviving textiles that can definitely be associated with Godwin.

Another furnishing fabric is a purple and green panel (p. 102) produced by Alexander Morton & Company, a leading textile firm in Darvel, Scotland. In its rigid symmetry and in many of its details, it recalls Renaissance velvets and silks, as well as Turkish textile patterns, especially the pointed-tulip motif. Nonetheless, the panel's production is totally modern: It was woven on a mechanized loom with silk and cotton, using gold and silver threads.

William Morris set up his weaving studio, along with workshops for other

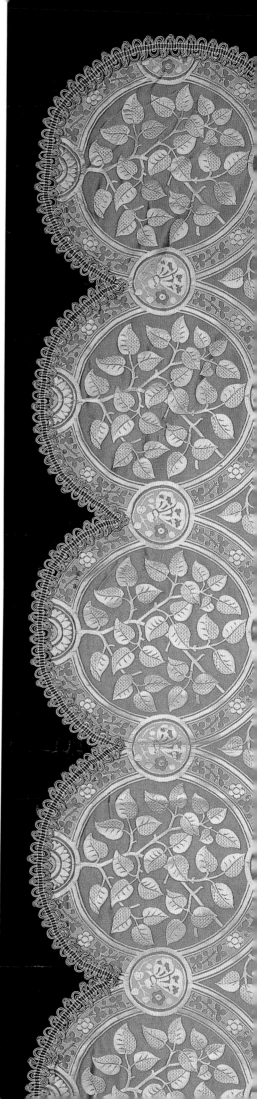

**Panel Entitled
"Large Syringa"**
Designed by
Edward William Godwin
England, London
Circa 1874

Panel
Designed by
Alexander Morton &
Company
Scotland, Darvel
1885/90

Hanging
Entitled "Pomona"
Designed by
Sir Edward Burne Jones
and William Morris
England, London, 1884/85
Woven at Merton Abbey
England, Wimbledon,
1898/1918

media, at Merton Abbey, in Wimbledon, in 1882. There, in collaboration with designer John Henry Dearle and Pre-Raphaelite painter Sir Edward Burne-Jones, he produced a small, tapestry-woven hanging entitled "Pomona" (p. 103). Burne-Jones provided the drawing for the goddess of the apple orchard. Her face, with its full features, and her heavily draped form reveal a sensuosity not found in the figures of the early Renaissance paintings that inspired it. The floral background is reminiscent of the famed millefleurs tapestries of the fifteenth and early sixteenth centuries, while the border design displays characteristics of early woodcuts. Made sometime between 1898 and 1918, "Pomona" and its companion piece, "Flora," were intended for home use. They are based on bigger versions which were, in fact, the first large tapestries to be woven at Merton Abbey, between 1884 and 1885.

Morris was responsible for a magnificent carpet (pp. 104–105) that was among the original furnishings of the John G. Glessner House, built by the architect Henry Hobson Richardson on Prairie Avenue in Chicago in 1886. For his carpets, Morris clearly studied Near Eastern prototypes. But his dense and rich designs, which achieve a remarkable balance between flat pattern and natural forms, are never imitative. The vibrantly colored carpet occupied a place of honor in the oak-paneled entrance hall of the Glessner House, along with portières, or door curtains, of woven wool. This curtain yardage — Morris's well-known "Peacock and Dragon" pattern, dating from 1878 — had impressed the Glessners when they saw it used in architect Richardson's own library.

Carpet
Designed by William Morris
England, London
Woven at Merton Abbey
England, Wimbledon
Early 1880s

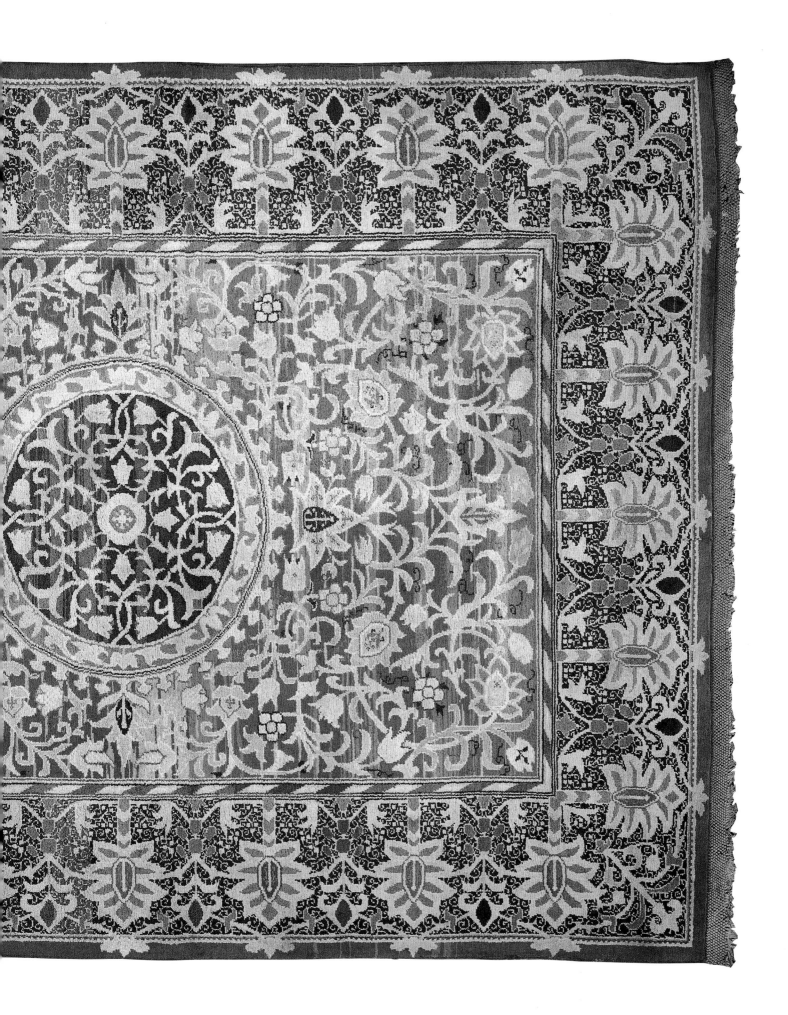

EARLIER AMERICAN TEXTILES

It is not surprising that earlier American textiles reflect the strong influence of European, especially English, designs and techniques. Materials were scarce and the making of utilitarian objects, such as bedcoverings, depended entirely on raw products that could be raised by a family or a community. Yet typical and indigenous forms of American needlework did develop, as can be seen in a masterful bed rugg (p. 107). Although the coiling tendrils of its design are reminiscent of motifs that appear in sixteenth- and seventeenth-century English textiles, their application to an item of bedcovering and the technique of looped running stitches (see separate entries in Glossary) embroidered through a woolen support fabric are typically American. The term *rugge* or *rugg* appears in colonial inventories, where it refers to a woven yardage fabric used to make bedcovers. These pieces were unique to the Connecticut River Valley. The information provided by the needlework contributes to the rarity of this piece: the initials H. J. refer to its maker, Hannah Johnson (1770–1848), daughter of Ebenezer and Ana Johnson. It is dated 1796 and carries the number 26, which tells us that Hannah Johnson was twenty-six years old when she made it.

Quilts, coverlets, and hooked rugs (see separate entries in Glossary) helped make cheerful the most modest interior. Among the easiest to fabricate was the sewn bedcover. Often worked in square sections, it could involve the participation of more than one person. The individual sections were completed at the various homes of those involved, and then everyone met at a quilting bee. There, the sections were joined, the batting (soft filling) and the backing fabric were assembled, and all three layers were interconnected under tension and quilted. The quilting bee was an occasion for conversation, eating, drinking, and dancing.

In superb condition is a friendship quilt (pp. 108, 109) made for Ella Maria Deacon. Many of the individual squares carry names written in sepia ink as well as an acrostic in the center of the bottom portion of the bedcover. To quote one line: "Methinks as [?] thy eye, o'er thy quilt warms with pleasure / Amid these mementoes, thou'll hold them a treasure." The cover was constructed through piecing (see Glossary) rather than appliquéing (see Glossary) or needleworking.

Another textile indigenous to the United States was the woven coverlet. The earlier coverlets were woven on four-harness looms (see Glossary). Sheep supplied the wool yarns, and flax, the linen, needed for the warp threads. Eventually, linen was replaced by cotton warps and, with the availability of the Jacquard attachment, simple looms could be converted to fashion large and complex coverlet patterns. Itinerant weavers such as James Cunningham traveled the countryside with such looms, as well as with pattern books, drafts (see Glossary), and tie-up diagrams (see Glossary). They lived temporarily with a community, for which they supplied coverlets in basic color combinations of blue and white (see p. 110) or red and white. Other color combinations existed as well, and, as commercial yarns became available, there was no limit to the colors that could be used. Customers would pick a pattern and often supplied wool, linen, or cotton that they had dyed themselves. The rest was done by weavers who would sign their name, and, occasionally, if the design permitted, an inscription and date. Often, in the signature block, weavers would include a symbol (such as a house, a lion, or a particular flower) to stand for their name. This eliminated the cumbersome job of having to weave it into every piece. As weavers traveled from place to place, so did their patterns. For that reason, identical coverlet patterns surface in more than one state. The coverlet illustrated here includes the patriotic sayings "United we stand / Divided we Fall" and "Under this we Prosper."

Originating in Europe, rug hooking enjoyed its greatest development in the United States. It developed in response to the demand in American homes for inexpensive floor coverings. Oriental carpets were too costly and, aside from skins, not much else was available. Any type of textile — old clothing, bedcovers, as well as yarns (unraveled or new) — could be recycled to make a hooked rug. Linen backing or even coffee, sugar, or feed bags were used as foundations, through which narrowly cut fabric strips were pulled with the aid of a hook, left in loops, and worked in rows.

Bed Rugg
Made by
Hannah Johnson
Connecticut,
Bozrah, 1796

Bedcover
New Jersey,
Mount Holly
1842

The date of 1776, featured in an important hooked rug (p. 111), is, of course, synonymous with the American colonies' irrevocable step toward independence. The rug includes other symbols of the formation of the United States: the Union Jack and an American flag with eight stars and ten stripes. The latter motif does not reflect the number of states at the time, but is, more likely, an instance of artistic license. Another date, 1861, included twice, commemorates the successful presidential campaign of Abraham Lincoln and his running mate, Hannibal Hamlin, both of whose initials are recorded.

As a sign of their prosperity and status, wealthy Americans throughout the eighteenth and nineteenth centuries ordered so-called fancy goods — silks for clothing and furniture coverings — chiefly from Europe. In the United States, silk manufacture was extremely limited. A superb and skillfully executed piece of cut and voided velvet (p. 112; see Glossary) was designed and woven by Gertrude Rapp, granddaughter of George Rapp, founder of the Harmonites, a separatist religious community that came to America from southern Germany in 1804. The community, which first settled in Pennsylvania, moved to Indiana, and returned to Pennsylvania, raised its own silkworms, an extraordi-

Fragment
Designed and woven
by Gertrude Rapp
Pennsylvania,
Old Economy
1830/50

nary accomplishment at the time. Rapp's design, which creates an optical illusion as if the fabric is rising and falling in several folds, is at once ingenious, sophisticated, and unique. This superb example of Harmonite work, which would have been fashioned into a garment to be worn only on festive occasions and on Sundays, equals the finest European velvet weaving of any period. In 1839, Gertrude Rapp was honored for "the best specimens of silk velvets and ribbons" and received a gold medal from the American Institute of New York for her work.

By the end of the eighteenth century, Americans had established businesses for the printing of textiles using engraved copper plates and rollers. Among the many factories developed along the Eastern seaboard, especially in New England, was the Merrimack Manufacturing Company, founded in 1823 at Lowell, Massachusetts, named for Francis Cabot Lowell, inventor of a power loom. Documenting the firm's skillful output is "Children at Play" (p. 113), based on a group of charming, anonymous engravings. The pattern, which was roller printed, is divided into sections to resemble a pieced quilt. The yardage would have been sold for a variety of uses — to be made into coverings or possibly even clothing.

Also roller printed are the 108 cotton rectangles showing flags from around the world, collected and sub-sequently worked by Theresa Zett Smith of Syracuse, New York, into a striking bedcover (pp. 114, 115). Known as "top sheets," these individual rectangles were originally placed inside the covers of wooden boxes in which tobacco and cigars were sold. Collected like baseball cards are today, top sheets were sewn together for pillows or bedcovers or were framed individually. The items they produced, although now objects of curiosity, were a genuine expression of popular art. Drawing on readily available, cheap materials, their makers put them together with flair and self-confidence.

**Fragment Depicting
Children at Play**
Massachusetts, Lowell
1886/90

COLUMBIA

BURMAH

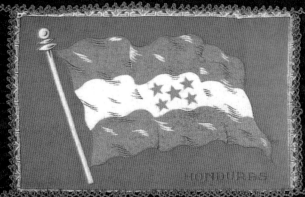

HONDURAS

CHINA (EMPIRE)

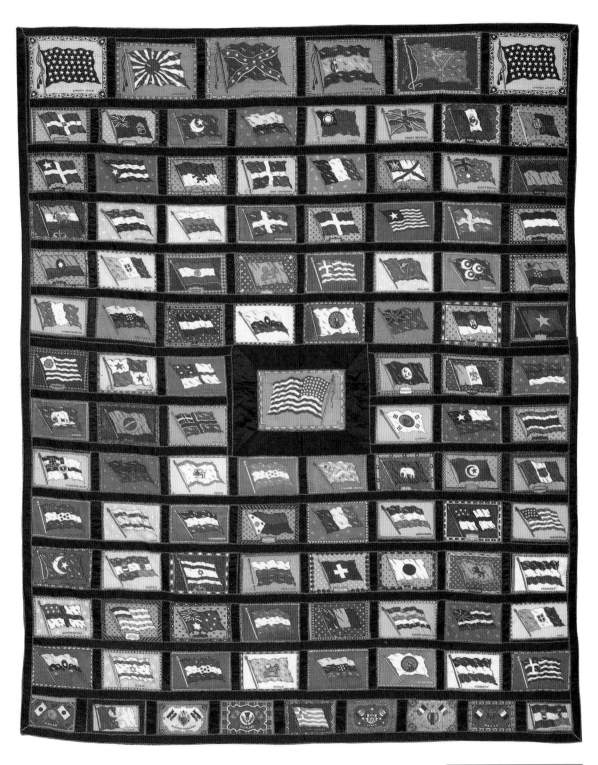

Bedcover with Cigar- or Tobacco-Box Rectangles
Made by Theresa Zett Smith
New York, Syracuse, 1913

Portière
Designed by
George Maher and
Louis J. Millet
United States, 1901

TEXTILES FOR CHICAGO INTERIORS

The drive for social reform in Chicago, led by Jane Addams at Hull House, made the city particularly receptive to the Arts and Crafts movement. Handicrafts were considered a way to encourage the craft traditions of growing immigrant populations and to enrich people's lives. Chicago's ties to the movement were cemented in the 1890s, with a number of events, not the least of which was the World's Columbian Exposition, hosted by the city in 1893. It included a display of the work of influential English architect-decorator Charles F. A. Voysey, among others. The department store Marshall Field & Company began to carry William Morris fabrics and carpets, which were used by architects who were creating residences being built for the city's prosperous business leaders.

The architecture of George Maher reflects the Prairie School style popularized by Frank Lloyd Wright, tempered by a Beaux-Arts classicism. With Louis J. Millet, Maher designed the James A. Patten house in Evanston, Illinois, in 1901. Maher, who met prominent Arts and Crafts figures on his travels in England, developed a design principle he called the "motif-rhythm theory," based on a theme —either abstract or natural forms— selected to unify a building's various elements. He chose a thistle as the motif for the Patten house. As photo-graphs of this building (demolished in 1938) show, thistle designs were employed repeatedly in stenciled wall decorations, leaded-glass windows, and fabrics such as the elegant portière on page 116.

In 1907, the Chicago Arts and Crafts Society, founded in 1897 by Wright and others, cosponsored with the Architectural League an exhibition of English and American arts and crafts at The Art Institute of Chicago. Its catalogue cover was designed by architect Louis H. Sullivan, whose firm had attracted a number of progressive young designers, including Wright and George Grant Elmslie. Born in Scotland, Elmslie joined the firm of Adler and Sullivan in 1895. While the medallion designs of a carpet from the Henry B. Babson House in Riverside, Illinois, are often referred to as "Sullivan-esque," Elmslie was actually responsible for most of the firm's decoration in the early years of the century. The original Babson House, designed by Sullivan's office in 1908–1909 under Elmslie's supervision, was altered in 1912 by Elmslie's own firm (formed in 1909). At this time, custom furnishings were added. Contemporary photo-graphs show a carpet (probably that seen at right), most likely produced during this period, in the first-floor hallway. It was probably manufactured for Elmslie in Europe.

Carpet
Designed by
George Grant Elmslie
United States, 1908/12

MODERN EUROPEAN YARDAGE

The Art Institute's textile collection is among the few that, as far back as the 1920s, has acquired twentieth-century yardage. Among the areas represented are textiles designed and manufactured at the Wiener Werkstätte (Vienna Workshop). The Werkstätte was founded in 1903 by architect and designer Josef Hoffmann and designer Koloman Moser, supported financially by Fritz Waerndorfer. It grew out of a movement that began in Vienna in 1897, when a number of artists, convinced that the arts in their city were stagnating, named themselves the "Secessionists" and instigated a vigorous program of exhibitions. They asked many foreign artists to participate, in order to reinvigorate the Viennese art scene with the new ideas that had first been introduced by the British Arts and Crafts movement. Active until 1932, the Werkstätte aimed to reinstate true craftsmanship and hand work, as well as to create functional designs that could be produced at prices the working classes could afford. Another goal of the group was to break down barriers between the fine and applied arts by training artists to work proficiently in a number of media. Thus, Werkstätte artists were equally adept at producing designs for architecture, ceramics, furniture, interiors, jewelry, leather work, metal work, and textiles.

While "Poppyheads" (*Mohnköpfe*) (pp. 118–19) was designed by Koloman

119

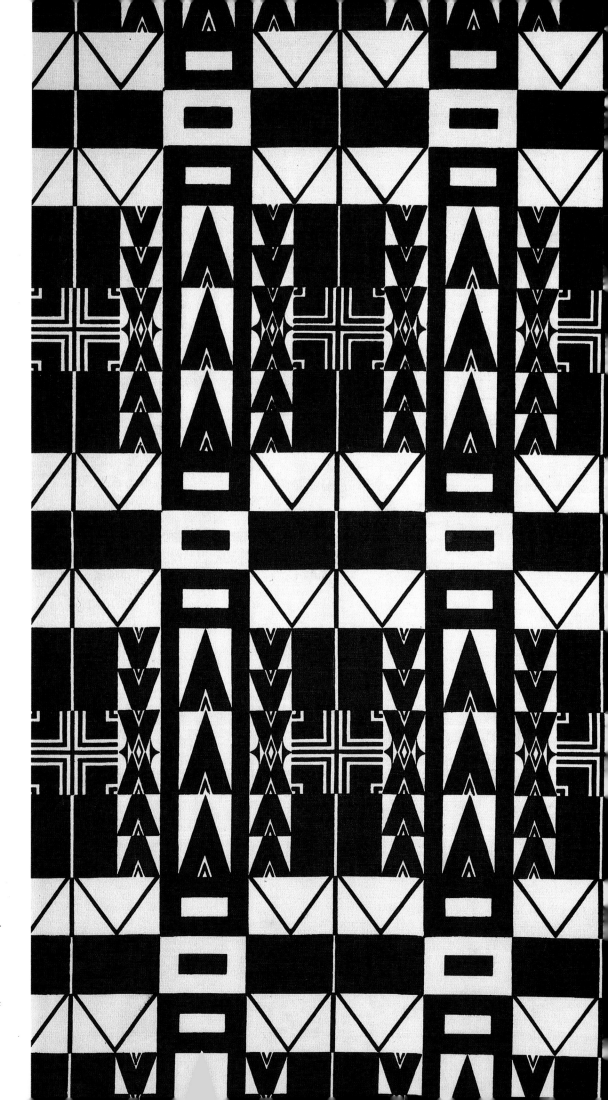

**Panel Entitled
"Santa Sofia"**
Designed by
Josef Hoffmann
Produced by the
Wiener Werkstätte
Austria, Vienna
1910/12

120

**Panel Entitled
"The Harvest"**
Designed by
Raoul Dufy
Produced by
Bianchini Ferier
France, Lyon
1920

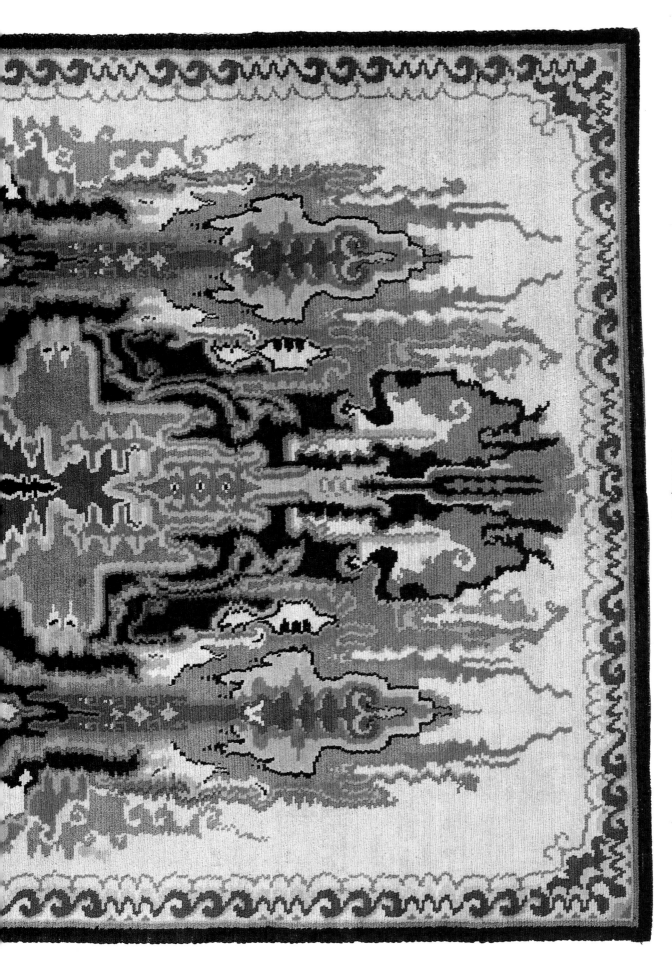

Carpet
Designed by
Jaap Gidding
The Netherlands
1920/25

Moser three years before the Werkstätte was formed, it demonstrates well the kind of elegant textile designs he was to produce at the Werkstätte. The pattern strongly reflects the influence of the French Art Nouveau movement in the fluidity of its organic forms, as well as in its combination of oranges and gold. It was produced in various colors by the Viennese firm of Johan Backhausen und Söhne, closely linked to the Werkstätte as its producer, and still in business today. The pattern was intended for upholstery or curtain fabric, ideally for rooms whose design and furnishings would be produced as total environments by Werkstätte artists.

"Santa Sofia" (p. 120), part of a series of textiles designed by Josef Hoffmann, reflects his architectural training in its striking geometry and in the gridlike character of its stark black-and-white pattern. The design, which was screen printed (see Glossary), reflects the goal of Hoffmann and his colleagues to create a simple, forthright, and abstract vocabulary that was progressive and modern, appropriate to the spirit of the new century. A sample book in the Oesterreichische Museum für Angewandte Kunst, Vienna, documents that the pattern was issued in several color schemes.

Contemporary trends in other European countries paralleled the Wiener Werkstätte's desire to reintroduce hand-controlled methods that would result in better design quality. In France, Raoul Dufy, best known today as a painter of cheerful Mediterranean scenes, was an energetic and highly versatile artist who deeply influenced European textile design in the second and third decades of this century. His application of sophisticated pictorial devices learned from Fauvism and Cubism, the two prime French artistic movements of his time, in combination with his deep appreciation of Oriental and medieval textiles, informed the nearly thirty thousand woodblock printed designs he is credited as having created in these years. Producing textiles in his own factory, Dufy was one of a number of artists whose work connected the worlds of avant-garde art and fashion. He worked with such firms as Chanel, Schiaparelli, and Bianchini-Ferier, for which he designed "The Harvest" (*La Moisson*; p. 121). This animated composition, comprising, in reversed repeats, a tractor driven by a farmer harvesting an abundant crop, closely resembles Dufy's bold work in another area, book illustration.

In Holland, Jacobus W. C. Gidding, a contemporary of painter Piet Mondrian and of architect and designer Gerrit Rietveld, created designs for many kinds of objects: art glass, ceram-

Border
Designed by Mariano Fortuny y Madrazo
Produced by the Società Anonima Fortuny
Italy, Venice, 1920/30

ics, and hangings. He also worked for various carpet and tapestry firms, including the Royal Carpet Manufactory in Rotterdam, producing designs for floor and table carpets, as well as hangings. In its bold colors and blurred forms, this luxurious carpet (pp. 122–23) manifests such diverse influences as Indonesian batiks, reflecting the centuries-old trading activity between the Netherlands and the Far East, and Dutch Art Nouveau designs.

Italian leadership in the production of velvets and silks was re-established in the 1920s primarily by two designers, Mariano Fortuny and Maria Monaci Gallenga. Fortuny, a Spanish painter who settled in Venice, found his sources of inspiration everywhere: in ancient garments from the Near East, Greece, and North Africa; in manuscript illuminations, paintings, and frescoes from Europe and Asia; in

Renaissance velvets, seventeenth-century lace, and Rococo silks. His dramatic clothing designs and elegant furnishing fabrics were enthusiastically acquired by a wealthy, international clientele. Intended as a furnishing fabric, the border on pages 124–25 echoes a seventeenth-century embroidered and appliquéd design and is rendered in a composite of techniques, including block printing and stenciling. Even today, the technical wizardry of the "Magician of Venice" — how he manipulated many processes simultaneously — is not fully understood.

Like Fortuny, the Roman designer Maria Monaci Gallenga used gold and silver pigments in her designs, ensuring the play of light over the surface and allowing subtle color variations. Gallenga's panel (p. 126), decorated with elongated tulip blossoms arranged in meandering garlands, was used as a furnishing fabric in her own residence. Its directness and simplicity recall the designs of sixteenth-century Ottoman fabrics, but its

regularized and sleek forms are part of the elegant formal vocabulary of the Art Deco movement of the 1920s.

Like the famed entrepreneur Sergei Diaghilev, for whose Ballets Russes he designed many celebrated sets and costumes, the Russian artist Leon Bakst was deeply influenced by the brilliant colors, simple outlines, and straightforward techniques used by Russian folk artists. A screen printed silk panel (p. 127) relates closely to designs Bakst devised as part of his only American commission, the 1922/23 conversion of the bowling alley of a private residence, the Evergreen House in Baltimore, into a theater. Among Bakst's fanciful motifs were colorful patterns applied to the theater's walls. He was in the United States that year for an exhibition of his work in New York and Chicago, where he also lec-

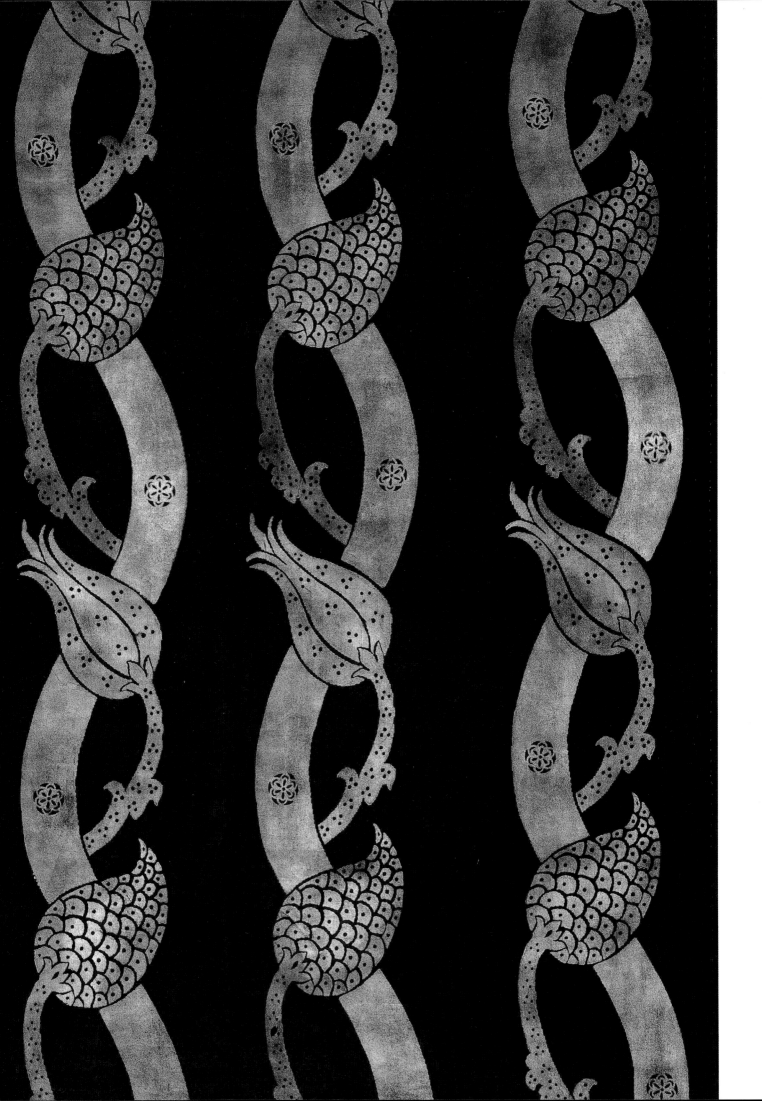

Panel
Designed by
Maria Monaci Gallenga
Produced by
the Atelier Gallenga
Italy, Rome, 1920/30

tured on textiles and costumes. Upon his return to Paris, Bakst apparently decided to reuse the theater motifs on lightweight silk fabrics intended for clothing. The Art Institute's panel, one of these patterns, presents an engaging mélange of Russian folk-art motifs and Art Deco patterns.

In Munich, Elisabeth Raab and Josef Hillerbrand were active in the Deutsche Werkstätten (German Workshops), whose members shared many of the ideals and goals of the Wiener Werkstätte. A noted teacher as well as a designer, Hillerbrand exerted enormous influence, touching a generation of German glassmakers, ceramists, metalworkers, as well as carpet, textile, and wallpaper designers. In designs such as that for a lace curtain (p. 129), Hillerbrand met the challenge to create materials that could be produced by machine more economically than labor-intensive handcrafted items. While traditional lace patterns were almost always floral or organic in design, Hillerbrand's lace curtain, of machine-woven cotton net enhanced by machine-embroidered motifs, exhibits a stark, architectural character that is quite appropriate to the industrial technology that made them. After studying with Hillerbrand, Raab joined the Werkstätten, for which she designed wallpapers and textiles. Her furnishing fabric (p. 128), with its clusters of floral sprigs spread over a white linen ground in a continuous repeat, was printed with several blocks to create a bright color palette.

Panel
Designed by
Leon Bakst, 1922/23
France, 1923/24

Panel
Designed by Elisabeth Raab
Produced by the Deutsche Werkstätten
Germany, Munich, 1920/27

Curtain Panel
Designed by Josef Hillerbrand
Produced by the Deutsche Werkstätten
Germany, Munich, 1920/27

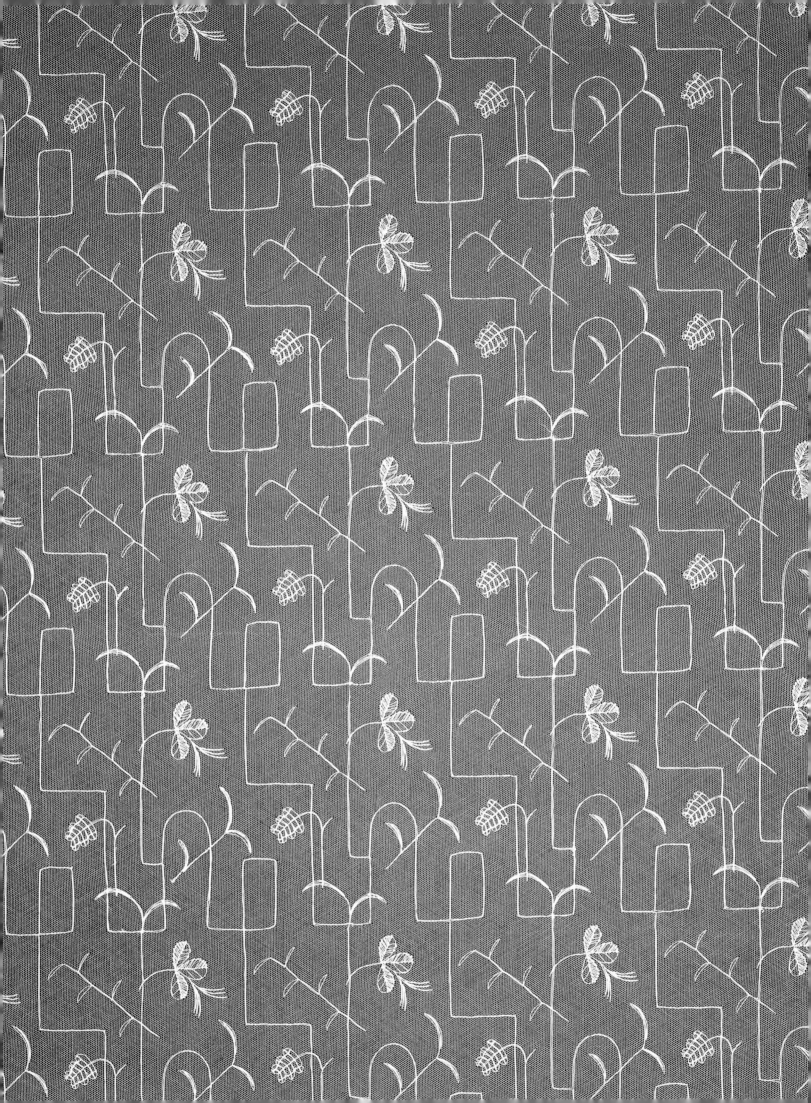

MODERN AMERICAN YARDAGE

While the Great Depression and World War II curtailed the textile industry that flourished in Europe through the 1920s and into the 1930s, the immigration to America of many artists and teachers sparked enormous interest in avant-garde ideas. At schools such as Black Mountain College (North Carolina), Cranbrook Academy of Art (outside Detroit), and the New Bauhaus/ Institute of Design (Chicago), world-renowned faculties, comprised largely of expatriates, introduced American students to radically new approaches to art and design, much of which was inspired by a single model: the Bauhaus.

This century's most important design school, the Bauhaus operated consecutively in three German cities — Weimar, Dessau, and Berlin — from 1919 to 1933, when it was forced to close. Decrying the separation of "structural and decorative arts," as its first director, Walter Gropius, put it, the Bauhaus embraced the machine as a positive, democratizing, and freeing force in the evolution of design. One of the school's directors, the revolutionary Hungarian artist Lazlò Moholy-Nagy, came to Chicago in 1937 to establish a school that promoted the tenets of the Bauhaus and served as an important link between Europe and America. Among the several styles Chicagoan Angelo Testa, a student of Moholy-Nagy's, developed for textiles, his geometric designs were greatly admired by his peers, especially architects and interior designers who had been frustrated in their search to find

contemporary American-designed fabrics that would complement the streamlined buildings they were creating. "Boston" (p. 132) takes its inspiration from the plan of this East Coast city, with all of its angular and asymmetrical features. Many conservative Bostonians considered the design too avant-garde, and, as a result, its sale in Boston was banned at the time it reached the market.

While Frank Lloyd Wright produced designs for a variety of interior elements — furniture, leaded windows, lighting fixtures, and carpets — he resisted designing yardage. However, by the mid-1950s, a number of his architectural plans had inspired a series of six printed and seven woven fabrics and four wallpapers. In 1955, the firm of F. Schumacher & Company issued "The Taliesin Line," named after Wright's residences and schools in Wisconsin and Arizona. "Design #104" (pp. 130–31) was derived from the plans of spherical houses for his sons Robert Llewellyn Wright and David Wright in Maryland and Arizona, respectively. Wright's love of elaborating on circular shapes is seen here in the interplay of spheres arranged in a highly charged, overall composition, which is further enhanced by subtle color choices: in this case, a palette of orange and white against gold. The screen printed (see Glossary) composition was offered in six color combinations and was continued until 1961.

Panel Entitled "Boston"
Designed by Angelo Testa
Printed by
Angelo Testa & Company
Illinois, Chicago, 1944

Panel Entitled "Bamako"
Designed and printed
by Charles Edmund
(Ed) Rossbach
California, Berkeley, 1960

In the post-war years, artists such as Charles Edmund (Ed) Rossbach became increasingly interested in exploring the expressive potential of forms, techniques, and materials of many pre-industrial cultures. Rather than strictly following these proto-types, however, Rossbach wandered freely among them, utilizing a variety of ancient techniques, sometimes simultaneously, or interpreting tradi-tional forms using unorthodox mate-rials, such as newspaper, plastic strips, and grass. In 1960, Rossbach wove a length of fabric as a prototype for cus-tom-designed yardage. In "Bamako" (p. 133), he used a dyeing process known as ikat (see Glossary). The piece's title refers to the capital of Mali, a country with a strong tradition of skilled ikat dyeing. Intended for the custom-tailored interior-design market, "Bamako" could be utilized as a wall or furniture fabric or be featured as an art object by stretching a length over a support and hanging it directly on the wall. "Bamako" was issued by the company of Jack Lenor Larsen, who had once served Rossbach as an assistant and who established an important textile-producing firm. While Rossbach has experimented pro-digiously over the past five decades with a number of forms, media, and styles, his oeuvre is harmonious in his emphasis on the aesthetic over the utilitarian, making him a pioneer of the fiber art movement.

The Other Land
(detail)
Lissy Funk
Switzerland, Zurich
1986–87
(Overall view on
pp. 140–41)

THE TEXTILE AS ART OBJECT

Far removed from yardage weaving is the one-of-a-kind piece with no, or relatively little, practical application. The trend toward liberating textiles from function so that they could assume the status of fine art began during the 1950s and was in full swing by the next decade. The movement was led by a number of outstanding American artists, including Lenore Tawney and Claire Zeisler.

The striking character of *Waters Above the Firmament* (pp. 136, 137) by Lenore Tawney owes to the simplicity of its basic concept, in which a large circle is set into a square. The piece's mystical quality is enhanced by the weight given to the upper half of the composition through the use of laminated strips of writing — not intended to be read — covered by an intense blue Liquitex paint. Tawney, known for her pioneering exposure of the warp, provides a variant on that theme. The circle is woven in a warp-faced, weft-ribbed plain weave (see separate entries in Glossary), with slits that open at regular, one-half-inch intervals. This creates a third dimension, a device Tawney has utilized in most of her weavings. Thus, her placement of a piece about one foot away from the wall creates a sense of space that is crucial to all her work. Trained in

sculpture at the Institute of Design in Chicago, Tawney has lived in New York since 1957. She is also known for her laminated boxes and collages, as well as for constructions composed of such materials as egg shells, chairs, or shoe forms. *Waters Above the Firmament* is the last and largest of Tawney's major weavings. In her most recent work, a series of gigantic "Clouds," she returned to the most basic element of textiles: the thread. In this series, thousands of linen threads are suspended dramatically from canvas supports attached to high ceilings.

Another artist who has enlarged the definition of art textiles is Luba Krejci. At the 1958 World's Fair in Brussels, she showed work that was a personal, contemporary interpretation of lace-making and lacis techniques. Never before had this medium been employed in such an abstract and whimsical way. Krejci, a teacher from Prague, studied archeology, ethnology, and textile design, and was connected with a program supporting folk art that operated in Czechoslovakia in the late 1950s and 1960s, all of which informed her art. In *Morpheus* (p. 138), a figure — perhaps the god of dreams himself — seems trapped, upside down, in a delicate net. Manipulating the black linen threads as a linear element, Krejci stretched them tautly from a black wooden frame, which becomes part of the composition. A white wall

surface plays an integral part of this piece, not only introducing contrast but also helping to make the threads appear as if they are floating in space, casting gentle shadows like a spider's web in a softly lighted room.

The noted Chicago artist Claire Zeisler was a sculptor who, working off the loom, handled fiber as others handle wood, metal, or stone. Her works explore the structure, suppleness, and strength of fibers through knotting, braiding, coiling, and piling. In *Private Affair I* (p. 139), a cascade of tightly knotted and wrapped strands of natural hemp falls into a whorl of loose ends that form the base. Its upright, frontal shape rises regally and silently. The simplicity of the natural hemp comprising the piece is enhanced by Zeisler's flawless craftsmanship, which was inspired by Pre-Columbian textile techniques and the American Indian woven baskets she collected throughout her life. Along with Tawney, Zeisler was instrumental in removing fiber pieces from their traditional place on the wall. By stressing the three-dimensionality of forms that she positioned, free-standing, on the floor, she empowered them to occupy space. The impact of *Private Affair I* derives, in the end, from its haunting, totemic presence.

Because the ancient technique of needlework is seldom used by artists today, due to its demanding and time-consuming requirements, it is remarkable to find a contemporary artist who has chosen to concentrate solely on that method, pushing it to new heights of scale and expression. Lissy Funk's *The Other Land (Das andere Land)* (pp. 135, 140–41) represents the Swiss artist's vision of the beyond and celebrates her expectations of the United States, created, as it was, for her first major museum retrospective exhibition, which opened at the Art Institute in 1988. Requiring the support of a wall, Funk's monumental pieces are conceived as abstract compositions. In this work, red curtains seem to have parted at the left and right, as well as at the top and bottom, to reveal a breathtaking panorama — a cosmic vision transporting the viewer to a wondrous, distant place. To create this technical and expressive tour de force, Funk and her assistants painstakingly applied silk threads and a variety of other fibers to a multilayered support, using standard needlework stitches. In a career stretching over sixty years, Funk has succeeded in expanding the potential of an ancient technique to embrace a twentieth-century mode of seeing.

**Waters Above
the Firmament**
Lenore Tawney
New York, New York
1976

137

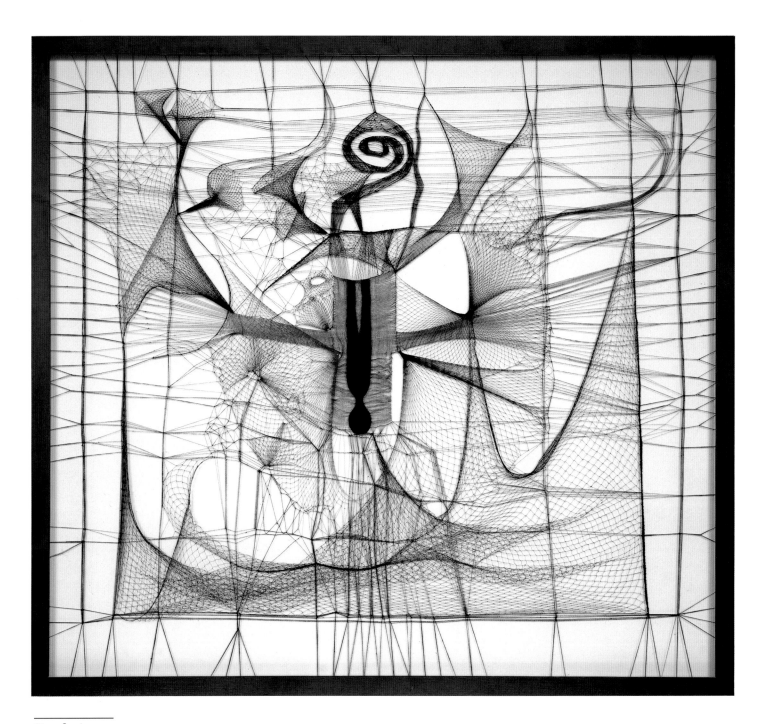

Morpheus
Luba Krejci
Czechoslovakia,
Prague, 1979

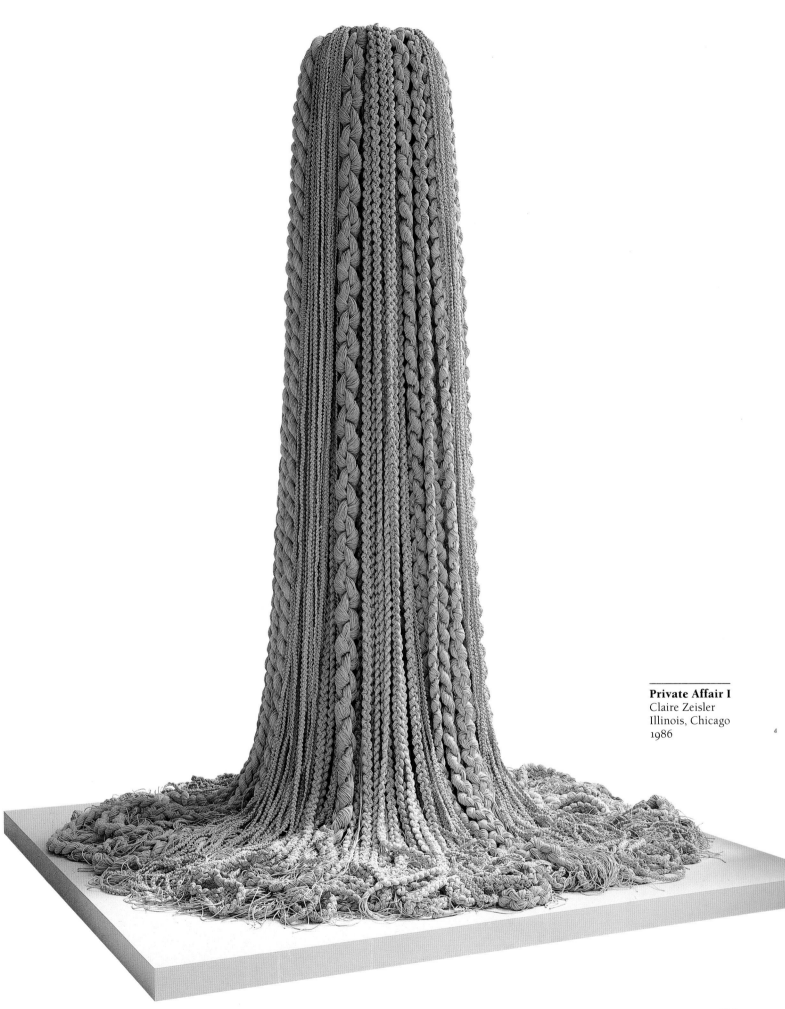

Private Affair I
Claire Zeisler
Illinois, Chicago
1986

139

CATALOGUE

Listed chronologically within chapters.
Page numbers of illustrations listed in italic.

COPTIC TEXTILES

Portion of Hanging with Warrior
Egypt, Coptic; fifth/sixth century
Linen and wool, plain weave with weft uncut pile and embroidered linen pile formed by variations in back and stem stitches
136.5 × 88.3 cm (53¾ × 34¾ in.)
Grace R. Smith Textile Endowment, 1982.1578
Pp. *10* (detail), *11*

Wide Border from Curtain or Hanging
Egypt, Coptic; sixth/eighth century
Linen and wool, slit and dovetailed tapestry weave with eccentric wefts and wrapped outlining wefts
129.8 × 19.2 cm (51 × 7⅝ in.)
repeat in warp direction: 56 cm (22 in.)
Ada Turnbull Hertle Endowment, 1972.366
Pp. *12–13* (detail), *13*

EARLY WESTERN SILKS

Fragment from Mantle of Doña Leonora, Wife of Don Felipe
Found in a tomb at Villacazar de Sirga, near Palencia
Kufic inscription: "Blessing"
Spain, late thirteenth century
Silk and gilt-animal-substrate-wrapped silk, weft-faced bands of plain weave with inner warps and complementary weft plain weave with inner warps
33.9 × 12.1 cm (13⅜ × 4¾ in.)
repeat in weft direction: 4.2 cm (1⅝ in.)
Restricted gift of Mrs. Chauncey B. Borland, 1950.1150
P. *15*

Fragment
Italy; thirteenth/fourteenth century
Silk and gilt-metal-strip-wrapped-silk, warp chevron twill weave with plain interlacings of secondary binding warps, and patterning and brocading wefts
22.95 × 30.4 cm (9 × 12 in.)
repeat in weft direction: 14.3 cm (5⅝ in.)
Gift of Mrs. Chauncey B. Borland, 1958.521
P. *16*

Fragment with Nazrid Coat of Arms
Kufic inscription: "Glory to our Lord the Sultan"
Spain; c. 1400
Silk and gilt-animal-substrate-wrapped silk, satin weave with plain interlacings of secondary binding warps and patterning wefts
42 × 19.7 cm (16½ × 7¾ in.)
repeat: 31.1 × 9.6 cm (12¼ × 3¾ in.)
Restricted gift of Mrs. Edwin A. Seipp, 1950.1149
P. *14*

Fragment
Egypt or Syria, Mamluk; fourteenth/fifteenth century
Silk, twill weave with plain interlacings of secondary binding warps and patterning wefts
23.5 × 29.4 cm (9¼ × 11½ in.)
repeat: 15.7 × 12.7 cm (6¼ × 5 in.)
Restricted gift of Mr. and Mrs. John V. Farwell III, 1982.1462
P. *17*

Panel
Italy, early fifteenth century
Silk, plain weave, cut solid velvet
49 × 59.7 cm (19¼ × 23⅝ in.)
repeat: 19.5 × 6 cm (7¾ × 2⅜ in.)
Kate S. Buckingham Endowment, 1954.12
P. *20*

Two Fragments
Kufic inscription: "I am for pleasure; for pleasure am I / he who beholds me sees joy and delight"
Spain; fifteenth century
Silk, satin weave with plain interlacings of secondary binding warps and patterning wefts
a: 53.4 × 27.3 cm (21 × 10 ¾ in.)
b: 51.5 × 18.6 cm (20¼ × 7⅝ in.)
repeat in warp direction: 17.8 cm (7 in.)
Restricted gift of the Needlework and Textile Guild of Chicago, 1945.216ab
Pp. *18, 19* (detail)

Altar Frontal
Italy; second half of fifteenth century
Silk, twill weave with twill interlacings of secondary binding warps and gilt-metal-strip-wrapped silk facing wefts forming weft loops in areas; cut, pile-on-pile voided velvet
100.8 × 203.4 cm (39¾ × 80 ⅛ in.)
repeat in warp direction: 84.4 cm (33¼ in.)
Kate S. Buckingham Endowment, 1944.403
P. *21*

LATER SILKS

Fragment
Italy; sixteenth century
Silk and gilt-metal strips, plain weave with patterning wefts
78.4 × 57.8 cm (30⅞ × 22¾ in.)
Restricted gift of Mr. and Mrs. John V. Farwell III, 1973.308
P. *24*

Panel
Italy; late sixteenth/early seventeenth century
Silk, plain weave with plain interlacings of secondary binding warps and patterning wefts
171.1 × 53.5 cm (67⅜ × 21⅛ in.)
repeat: 33.3 × 17.1 cm (13 × 6¾ in.)
Bequest of Mr. and Mrs. Martin A. Ryerson, 1937.1215
Pp. *22–23*

Hood from Cope with Heraldic Attributes of Santiago, Castile, and Leon
Spain; seventeenth century
Silk and gilt-metal-strip-wrapped silk, satin damask weave with brocading wefts
52 × 50.6 cm (20⅜ × 19⅞ in.)
repeat in warp direction: 34 cm (13⅜ in.)
Restricted gift of Mrs. Chauncey B. Borland, 1945.162
P. *25*

GLORY TO GOD: ALTARPIECES AND CHASUBLES

Chasuble Front with Orphrey Cross
Chasuble: Italy, Florence; fifteenth century
Orphrey cross: Bohemia or Germany; first half of fifteenth century
Chasuble: silk, plain weave with silk facing wefts, twill interlacings of secondary binding warps and gilt-metal-strip-wrapped silk facing wefts forming weft loops in areas, cut pile-on-pile voided velvet
Orphrey cross: linen, plain weave; embroidered with silk and gilt-and-silvered-animal-substrate-wrapped linen in bullion, outline, satin, and split stitches; laid work, couching, and padded couching; edged with woven fringe and tapes
Chasuble: 126.6 × 70.5 cm (49⅞ × 27¾ in.)
Orphrey cross: 112.2 × 57.7 cm (44⅛ × 22¾ in.)
Grace R. Smith Textile Endowment, 1980.615
Pp. *26* (detail), *27*

**Retable Depicting the
Madonna and Child, Nativity,
and Adoration of the Magi;
Altar Frontal with the
Resurrection and Six Apostles**
Made for Pedro de Montoya, Bishop of Osma
from 1454 to 1475
Spain, Burgo de Osma; c. 1468
Linen, plain weave; appliquéd with linen and
silk, plain weave; silk, plain weave; and cut
solid velvet
Retable: embroidered with silk floss and
creped yarns, gilt-and-silvered-metal-strip-
wrapped silk in brick, bullion, chain, split,
stem, and a variety of satin stitches; laid work,
couching, and padded couching; seed pearls
and spangles
Altar frontal: embroidered with linen, silk,
gilt-metal-strip-wrapped silk in satin and split
stitches; laid work, couching, and padded
couching; spangles
Retable: 165.2 × 200.8 cm (65 × 79 in.)
Altar frontal: 88.8 × 202.3 cm
(35 × 79⅝ in.)
Gift of Mrs. Chauncey McCormick and Mrs.
Richard Ely Danielson, 1927.1779
Pp. *28, 29* (detail)

**Altar Frontal
Depicting Scenes from
the Life of Christ**
Made for the Cathedral Seo de Urgel
Spain, Leridà Province; late sixteenth century
Silk, broken warp chevron twill weave, cut solid
velvet; appliquéd with linen, plain weave; silk
and gilt and silvered wire, plain weave with
twill interlacings of secondary binding warps
and patterning wefts; silk and gilt and silvered
wire, twill weave; embroidered with silk, gilt-
and-silvered-metal-strip-wrapped silk, and gilt
and silvered wire in overcast satin, padded satin,
split, and stem stitches; laid work, couching
and padded couching; semiprecious stones;
edged with woven fringes
106.7 × 237 cm (42 × 93¼ in.)
Restricted gift of Mrs. Chauncey McCormick
and Mrs. Richard Ely Danielson, 1944.623
Pp. *30* (detail), *31*

TAPESTRIES FOR
CHURCH AND CASTLE

Hanging Depicting the Annunciation
Inscription: *A[ve] G[ratia] P[lena] Ecce Ancilla
D[omini] F[iat] M[ihi] S[ecundum] T[uum]*
("Hail full of grace; behold the handmaid of the
Lord; Be it unto me according to Thy Word")
Made for Giovanni Francesco Gonzaga II, Duke
of Mantua (1466–1519)
Design attributed to Andrea Mantegna (Italian;
1431–1506) or artists at court of Mantua
Italy, Mantua; 1506/19
Wool, silk, and gilt-and-silvered-metal-strip-
wrapped silk, slit, dovetailed, and interlocking
tapestry weave
178.8 × 114.6 cm (70⅜ × 45⅛ in.)
Bequest of Mr. and Mrs. Martin A. Ryerson,
1937.1099
Pp. *32, 33* (detail)

Hanging Depicting the Holy Family
Flanders, early sixteenth century
Linen, wool, silk, and gilt-metal-strip-wrapped
silk, slit tapestry weave
75.6 × 68.2 cm (29¾ × 26⅞ in.)
Bequest of Mr. and Mrs. Martin A. Ryerson,
1937.1097
Pp. *34, 35* (detail)

TEXTILES FOR DAILY LIFE

Antependium Section Depicting
the Last Supper
Germany, 1300/10
Linen, plain weave; pulled thread work embroidered with silk and linen in chained border,
overcast, and two-sided Italian cross stitches;
embroidered with silk and linen in satin, single
satin, stem, and stem filling stitches; couching;
edged with woven tape
38.3 × 39.4 cm (15⅛ × 15½ in.)
Purchased from the Field Museum of Natural
History, 1907.765
P. *37*

Towel
Italy, Perugia; fifteenth century
Linen, bands of diamond twill weave and plain
weave with patterning wefts
231.6 × 58.15 cm (91³⁄₁₆ × 22⅞ in.)
Gift of the Antiquarian Society of The Art
Institute of Chicago, 1899.8
P. *40*

Hanging Entitled "The Lovers"
Inscription: *ich spil mit uch in truwe; des sol uch
niemer ruwen*
("I love you faithfully; I hope you will never
regret it")

Switzerland, Basel; 1490/1500
Linen, wool, and silk, slit and double
interlocking tapestry weave
105.3 × 78.9 cm (41½ × 31⅛ in.)
Gift of Kate S. Buckingham, 1922.5378
Pp. *38–39*

Panel Depicting Christ
Entering Jerusalem
Denmark, Schleswig-Holstein; seventeenth
century
Linen and wool, plain weave with plain interlacings of secondary binding warps and
patterning wefts
167.4 × 83.2 cm (65⅞ × 32¾ in.)
repeat: 74.6 × 63.5 cm (29⅜ × 25 in.)
Bequest of Hans G. Cahen, 1984.1068
P. *41*

THE SPLENDOR OF VESTMENTS

Cope
England; late fifteenth/early sixteenth century
Silk, broken warp chevron twill weave; cut
voided velvet; appliquéd with linen, plain
weave; embroidered with silk, gilt-metal-strip-
wrapped silk in satin and split stitches; laid
work, couching, and padded couching; spangles
144 × 291.1 cm (56¾ × 114⅝ in.)
Grace R. Smith Textile Endowment, 1971.312a
Pp. *42, 43* (detail)

Chasuble Depicting the Baptism of Christ
After fresco by Andrea del Sarto (Italian; 1486–
1530) in the Chiastro della Scalzo, Florence
Italy; medallion: after 1517
Chasuble: early seventeenth century
Linen, plain weave with inset medallion of
silk, satin weave embroidered with silk
and gilt-and-silvered-metal-strip-wrapped
silk and linen in satin, split, and stem
stitches; couching and French knots; edged
with woven tape
109.5 × 73.3 cm (43⅛ × 28⅞ in.)
Grace R. Smith Textile Endowment, 1971.313
Pp. *44, 45* (detail)

Cope
Spain, seventeenth century
Linen, plain weave; embroidered with silk
floss in satin, padded satin, and split stitches;
laid work and couching

149.8 × 303.75 cm (59 × 119½ in.)
Gift of Mr. and Mrs. Harold Henderson, 1970.1081
Pp. *46–47*

Chasuble
Italy or Sicily; early/mid-seventeenth century
Silk, satin weave; embroidered with linen, silk, gilt-metal strips, and gilt-metal-strip-wrapped silk in satin and split stitches; couching and padded couching; beaded with coral
113.5 × 66.8 cm (44⅝ × 26¼ in.)
Restricted gift of Mr. and Mrs. John V. Farwell III, 1965.773
Pp. *48–49*

Chasuble
France, early eighteenth century
Silk and gilt-metal-strip-wrapped silk, satin damask weave with brocading wefts; edged with woven fringe
110.6 × 74.4 cm (43½ × 29¼ in.)
Royalties from The Warner Company, 1982.1388
P. *51*

Cope with Self-Orphrey Band
France, c. 1765
Silk and silk chenille yarns, plain weave with patterning warps and brocading wefts; edged with woven tape
135.1 × 276.7 cm (53⅛ × 109 in.)
Gift of Mrs. Chauncey McCormick and Mrs. Richard Ely Danielson, 1948.142
Pp. *52–53*

THE LARGE PICTORIAL HANGING

Tapestry of a type known as "Verdure de Bocages et de Bêtes Savages"
Southern Netherlands (now Belgium), Hainault, Tournai; first half of sixteenth century
Wool, slit, single dovetail, and double interlocking tapestry weave
594.4 × 333.4 cm (231½ × 131¼ in.)
Gift of the Antiquarian Society of The Art Institute of Chicago through the Jessie Landon Fund, 1934.4
Pp. *55* (detail) *56–57*

Table Carpet Depicting Scenes from the Life of Christ
Northern Netherlands, 1600/50
Linen, wool, and silk, slit and double interlocking tapestry weave
264.8 × 163.2 cm (1046¼ × 64¼ in.)
Ada Turnbull Hertle Endowment, 1978.58
Pp. *58* (detail), *59*

Hanging Entitled "The Tamers" (*Les Dompteurs*) from the "Grotesques" Series
Designed by Jean Baptiste Monnoyer (?) (French; 1636–1699) in the style of Jean Bérain I (French; 1640–1711); woven under Philippe Behagle (French; 1641–1705)
France, Beauvais; late seventeenth/early eighteenth century
Wool and silk, slit and double interlocking tapestry weave
257.1 × 309.8 cm (180¼ × 122 in.)
Gift of Robert Allerton, 1956.101
Pp. *60*, *61* (detail)

Hanging Entitled "Autumn"
After a cartoon by Charles Le Brun (French; 1619–1690); woven by Etienne Claude Le Blond (French; c. 1700–1751) and Jean de La Croix (French; active 1662–1712) at the Gobelins Manufactory
France, Paris; c. 1710
Wool and silk, slit and double interlocking tapestry weave
531.8 × 378.8 cm (209⅜ × 149⅛ in.)
Gift of the Hearst Foundation, 1954.260
Pp. *62* (detail), *63*

ENGLISH NEEDLEWORK

Panel
England, sixteenth century
Linen, plain weave; embroidered with silk, gilt-metal-strip-wrapped silk in Algerian eye, back, buttonhole, open buttonhole filling, chain, double running, running, overcast, plaited braid, and square openwork stitches; laid work, couching, and woven wheels; spangles
73.9 × 61.5 cm (29⅛ × 24¼ in.)
Restricted gift of Mrs. Chauncey B. Borland, 1955.1221
P. *65*

Cushion Cover (one of a pair)
Inscriptions: *N W / 1601 / C W*
England; 1601
Linen, plain weave; embroidered with silk, linen, and wool in long-armed cross stitches; edged with woven fringe
49.5 × 52.8 cm (19½ × 20¾ in.)
Robert Allerton Endowment, 1989.149
P. *66*

Bedcover
England; c. 1620
Linen and cotton, twill weave; embroidered with wool in Algerian eye, back, individual back, crossed back, buttonhole, pearl, Romanian, running, individual running, individual satin, stem, and two-sided Italian cross stitches; couching; edged with woven tape
159.6 × 134.8 cm (62¾ × 53 in.)
Robert Allerton Endowment, 1986.988
P. *67*

Panel
England; late seventeenth century
Cotton and linen, twill weave; embroidered with wool and silk in back, bullion, buttonhole, chain, detached chain, coral, satin, single satin, and stem stitches; laid work, couching, and French knots
190.5 × 94.5 cm (75 × 37¼ in.)
Restricted gift of Mrs. Chauncey B. Borland, 1964.188
Pp. *68, 69* (detail)

Bedcover
England; c. 1720
Cotton, plain weave; embroidered with silk in back, cross, herringbone, individual satin, satin, star, and stem stitches; laid work, couching, and French knots
155.9 × 147.8 cm (61⅜ × 58⅛ in.)
Restricted gift of Mr. and Mrs. John V. Farwell III, 1985.84a
Pp. *70* (detail), *71*

NEEDLEWORK OBJECTS

Unassembled Woman's Coif
England; c. 1600
Linen, plain weave; embroidered with silk and gilt-and-silvered-metal-strip-wrapped silk in back, individual back, bullion, chain, plaited braid, and stem stitches; couching, darned wheels, and French knots
24.9 × 41.1 cm (9¾ × 16⅛ in.)
Gift of Mrs. Chauncey B. Borland, 1948.90
P. *72*

**Mirror Depicting
Charles II (?) and
Catherine of Braganza (?)
and Old Testament Figures**
England; c. 1665
Silk, satin weave; embroidered with silk,
silk-wrapped gilt-metal strip, purl, and card-
board in overcast, running, satin, and split
stitches; raised work in brick stitches; laid
work, couching, padded couching, and French
knots; braided pompons, and seed pearls; in
tortoiseshell frame
101.9 × 74.1 cm (40⅛ × 29¼ in.)
Gift of Mrs. Laurance H. Armour, Jr. in memory
of her mother, Mrs. Henry Malcolm Withers,
1963.748
Pp. *74, 75* (detail)

**Casket Depicting
Scenes from the
Old Testament**
Inscriptions: *R.S. / I.P. / 1668 / R.S.*
Made by Rebecca Stonier Plaisted
England; 1668
Silk, satin weave; embroidered with silk and
silk-wrapped-metal purl in brick, bullion,
Ceylon, chain, knot, lattice filling, overcast,
running, satin, Smyrna cross, tent, and a variety
of buttonhole stitches; laid work, couching, and
padded couching, French and Turkey knots;
applied areas of linen, plain weave; and silk
fringe; seed pearls, coral beads, and mica; edged
with woven tape
39 × 38.3 × 29 cm (15⅜ × 15 × 11½ in.)
Restricted gift of Mrs. Chauncey B. Borland and
Mrs. Edwin A. Seipp, 1959.337
P. *73*

Panel from Settee
England or France; mid-eighteenth century
Linen, plain weave; embroidered with silk and
wool in tent stitch
76 × 191.3 cm (29⅞ × 75⅜ in.)
Royalties from The Warner Company; restricted
gift of Mr. and Mrs. Don H. Reuben and the
Needlework and Textile Guild of Chicago,
1982.199
Pp. *76–77*

THE MAGIC OF LACE

Border Made Into a Collar
Italy; late sixteenth/early seventeenth century
Linen, three bands of plain weave; cut work
filled with needle lace; edged with bobbin
straight-lace
22.1 × 150.3 cm (8¾ × 59¼ in.)
Gift of the Antiquarian Society of The Art
Institute of Chicago, 1937.451
Pp. *78* (detail), *79*

Cover
France; 1620/30
Linen, twenty-four squares of square netting
alternating with twenty-four squares of plain
weave; cut and drawn work appliquéd with
plain weave; embroidered in back, bullion,
cloth, cross, darning, half cross, detached chain,
double running, twined double running, running, interlocking lace, overcast, satin, single
and surface satin and stem stitches; eyelet holes,
knots and French knots; overcast bars, button-
holed, darned, and woven wheels; needle lace
filling stitches; edged with bobbin straight-lace
105.3 × 137.3 cm (41½ × 54 in.)
Grace R. Smith Textile Endowment, 1986.11
Pp. *80–81*

Border Fragment
Inscriptions: *Vive Le Roi* ("Long live the King");
Carolus Rex ("King Charles") *C B Baronet*
(Sir Copleston Bampfield [1638–1692])
C 1661 B
England, Devonshire, Dorset; 1661
Linen, bobbin part-lace
23⅝ × 5⅛ in (60 × 13 cm)
Gift of the Antiquarian Society of The Art
Institute of Chicago, 1937.452b
Pp. *82–83*

Cravat End with Monogram of Louis XIV
Belgium, Brussels; 1700/15
Linen, bobbin part-lace of a type known
as "Brussels"
32.1 × 41.7 cm (12⅝ × 16⅜ in.)
Restricted gift of Mr. and Mrs. John V. Farwell
III, 1987.334
P. *84*

**Veil with Russian Imperial Family Coat
of Arms**
Belgium; late nineteenth century
Cotton, needle lace of a type known as "Point
de Gaze"
225 × 183.6 cm (88½ × 72¼ in.)
Gift of Mrs. Potter Palmer, Sr., through the
Antiquarian Society of The Art Institute of
Chicago, 1924.40
P. *85*

SILKS FROM FRANCE
AND ENGLAND

Panel
France; c. 1734
Silk, silvered-metal strips, and gilt-and-silvered-
metal-strip-wrapped silk, plain weave with twill
interlacings of secondary binding warps and
some brocading wefts
79.4 × 55.3 cm (31¼ × 21¾ in.) repeat in warp
direction: 60.8 cm (23⅞ in.)
Restricted gift of the Textile Society of The Art
Institute of Chicago, 1980.122
P. *87*

Panel
France, Lyon; c. 1735
Silk, satin weave with twill interlacings
of brocading and some self-patterning ground
wefts and plain interlacings of secondary
binding warps and some self-patterning
ground wefts
106.6 × 54.3 cm (42 × 21⅜ in.)
repeat: 41 × 26.7 cm (16⅛ × 10½ in.)
Gift of Mrs. Chauncey B. Borland, 1955.809
P. *86*

Panel
Designed by Anna Maria Garthwaite (?)
(English; 1720–1756)
England, London, Spitalfields; 1741/42
Silk, plain weave with twill interlacings of
secondary binding warp and brocading wefts
107.8 × 52.7 cm (42⅜ × 20¾ in.)
repeat in warp direction: 92.3 cm (36⅜ in.)
Restricted gift of Mr. and Mrs. John V. Farwell
III and Miss Mildred Davison in honor of Mrs.
Chauncey B. Borland, 1971.646c
P. *88*

Panel
Woven for the summer palace of Empress
Catherine II of Russia, Tsarskoe Selo
Designed by Philippe de LaSalle (French;
1723–1805); woven and produced by Camille
Pernon & Cie
France, Lyon; c. 1775
Silk and linen, satin weave with brocading
wefts; painted details
192.4 × 54.8 cm (75¾ × 21⅝ in.)
repeat in warp direction: 87.3 cm (34⅜ in.)
Restricted gift of the Textile Society of The Art
Institute of Chicago, 1983.748
P. *92*

Panel
Designed by Claude Camille Pierre Pernon
(French; 1735–1808); woven and manufactured
by Camille Pernon & Cie
Made for the Salon de Velours at the Casita del
Principe, Pardo Palace, near Spain
France, Lyon; 1788
Silk, twill weave cut solid velvet; pile warp
printed technique known as "chiné"
331.8 × 55.8 cm (130⅝ × 21⅞ in.)
repeat in warp direction: 57.5 cm (22⅝ in.)
Grace R. Smith Textile Endowment, 1990.212
P. 89

Panel
France, Lyon; c. 1790
Silk, satin weave with plain interlacings of
secondary binding warps and self-patterning
ground wefts
227.8 × 55.2 cm (89⅝ × 21¾ in.)
repeat in warp direction: 110.4 cm (43⅜ in.)
Belle M. Borland Endowment, 1982.7
P. 91

**Panel Entitled "The Pheasants" from the
"Verdures of the Vatican" Series**
Designed by Jean Démosthène Dugourc
(French; 1749–1825); woven and manufactured
by Camille Pernon & Cie
Made for the Casita del Labrador, near
Madrid, Spain
France, Lyon; after 1799
Silk, satin weave with plain interlacings of
secondary binding warps and brocading wefts;
embroidered with silk in chain (tambour
work) and satin stitches
242.5 × 44.5 cm (95¼ × 17½ in.)
Restricted gift of Mrs. Chauncey B. Borland,
1945.12
P. 90

Panel
Woven and produced by Mathevon et Bouvard
France, Lyon; 1860/80
Silk, satin weave with twill interlacings of
secondary binding warps and patterning and
brocading wefts
192.2 × 77.9 cm (75⅝ × 30⅝ in.)
repeat in warp direction: 167.3 cm (65⅞ in.)
Restricted gift of the Antiquarian Society of
The Art Institute of Chicago, 1988.526
P. 93

THE PRINTED CLOTH

**Panel Entitled
"A Visit to the Camp"**
Inscription: *Royal Artillery / G III R*
After satirical engravings of Henry Bunbury
(English; 1750–1811)
England, c. 1785
Cotton, plain weave; copperplate printed
90.9 × 70.4 cm (35¾ × 27¾ in.)
repeat in warp direction: 84 cm (33 in.)
Gift of Emily Crane Chadbourne,
1952.585a
P. 95

Panel
Designed by Jean Baptiste Huet (French;
1745–1811)
France, Nantes; c. 1786
Linen, plain weave; copperplate printed
274 × 99.1 cm (107⅞ × 39 in.)
repeat in warp direction: 92.2 cm (36¼ in.)
Gift of Robert Allerton, 1924.499
P. 96

**Panel Entitled
"The Flowering Cornucopia"
(La Corne fleurie)**
Printed and produced by J. P. Meillier et Cie
France, Bordeaux, Beautiran; after 1789
Cotton, plain weave; block printed
82.5 × 101.1 cm (32½ × 39¾ in.)
repeat: 40.8 × 93.2 cm (16⅛ × 36⅝ in.)
Gift of Robert Allerton, 1925.729
P. 97

**Panel Entitled
"The Merchant of Love"
(La Marchande d'Amour)**
Designed by Louis Hippolyte LaBas (French;
1782–1867); printed and produced by Chris-
tophe Philippe Oberkampf (French; 1738–1815)
France, Jouy-en-Josas; 1815/1817
Cotton, plain weave; engraved roller printed
99 × 95.2 cm (39 × 37½ in.)
repeat in warp direction: 49.8 cm (19¾ in.)
Gift of Mrs. Lawrence McClure, 1966.146
P. 98

Panel
Printed and produced by Lancaster Prints
England; 1856
Cotton, plain weave; engraved roller printed;
glazed
544.8 × 60.7 cm (214½ × 23⅞ in.)
repeat in warp direction: 40.6 cm (16 in.)
Restricted gift of Mrs. Homer Dixon, 1958.762
P. 99

REVIVAL AND REFORM MOVEMENTS

Panel Entitled "Large Syringa"
Designed by Edward William Godwin (English;
1833–1886); woven and produced by Warner &
Sons, Limited
England, London; c. 1874
Silk, satin damask weave; edged with cotton
and silk, plain weave cut solid velvet, and
woven tape
334.3 × 182.7 cm (131½ × 72 in.)
repeat: 26.3 × 26.3 cm (10⅜ × 10⅜ in.)
Grace R. Smith Textile Endowment, 1987.333
Pp. 100–101

Panel
Designed, woven, and produced by Alexander
Morton & Company
Scotland, Darvel; 1885/90
Silk, cotton, and gilt-and-silvered-metal-strip-
wrapped cotton, satin weave with twill inter-
lacings of secondary binding warps and
patterning wefts
248.1 × 129.5 cm (97⅝ × 51 in.)
repeat: 103.3 × 64.2 cm (40⅝ × 25¼ in.)
Ada Turnbull Hertle Endowment, 1988.106
P. 102

Carpet
From the John J. Glessner House, Chicago
Designed by William Morris (English; 1834–
1896); woven and produced by Morris &
Company, Merton Abbey
England, Surrey, Wimbledon; early 1880s
Cotton and wool, plain weave with "Ghiordes
knots" cut pile
472.3 × 333.4 cm (186 × 131¼ in.)
Gift of Mrs. Charles F. Batchelder, 1974.524
Pp. 104–105

Hanging Entitled "Pomona"
Designed by Sir Edward Burne-Jones (English;
1833–1898) and William Morris (English;
1834–1896), England, London; 1884–85;
woven and produced by William Morris
Workshop, Merton Abbey
England, Surrey, Wimbledon; 1898/1918
Cotton, wool, and silk, double interlocking
tapestry weave
92.9 × 165.1 cm (36½ × 65 in.)
Ida E. Noyes Fund, 1919.792
P. 103

EARLIER AMERICAN TEXTILES

Bed Rugg
Inscription: *H J 26 / 1796*
Made by Hannah Johnson (American;
1770–1848)
Connecticut, New London County, Bozrah;
1796
Wool, plain weave; embroidered with wool
yarns in looped running stitches, cut to
form pile
249.4 × 246.1 cm (98¼ × 97 in.)
Gift of the Needlework and Textile Guild of
Chicago, 1944.27
P. *107*

Bedcover
Made for Ella Maria Deacon (1811-1894)
New Jersey, Mount Holly; 1842
Cotton, plain weaves; pieced and appliquéd
with cotton, plain weaves, some printed in
a variety of techniques, some glazed; quilted
264.7 × 272.6 cm (104⅛ × 107⅜ in.)
Gift of Mrs. Betsey Leeds Tait Puth, 1978.923
Pp. *108–109* (detail)

Coverlet
Inscriptions: *1843 United We Stand Divided We
Fall/Washington/Under This We Prosper/
J Cunningham Weaver/New Hartford/Oneida
Co/N York*
Woven by James Cunningham (American;
c. 1797–?)
New York, Oneida County, New Hartford; 1843
Cotton and wool, plain weave double cloth; two
loom widths joined
228.8 × 184.9 cm (90 × 72¾ in.)
Gift of Emily Crane Chadbourne, 1930.111
P. *110*

Fragment
Designed by Gertrude Rapp (American; 1808–
1889); woven and produced by the Harmonites
Society
Pennsylvania, Ambridge, Old Economy;
1830/50
Silk, satin weave with patterning warps, cut
voided velvet
24.4 × 47 cm (9⅝ × 18½ in.)
repeat: 11.6 × 5.1 cm (4⅝ × 2 in.)
Acquired by exchange from the Scalamandré
Museum, New York, 1952.502
P. *112*

Rug
Inscriptions: *1861 / 1776 / AB. LI. /HA. HA./
MAY ACO*
United States, after 1861
Linen, plain weave with cotton and wool strips
of plain and twill weaves forming "hooked"
pile; edged with cotton, twill weave tape
99 × 180.4 cm (39 × 71 in.)
Bequest of William McCormick Blair, 1984.1087
P. *111*

Fragment Depicting Children at Play
Printed and produced by Merrimack Company
Massachusetts, Lowell; 1886/90
Cotton, plain weave; engraved roller printed
66 × 48.2 cm (26 × 19 in.)
repeat in warp direction: 21.35 cm (8⅜ in.)
Gift of Mrs. Chauncey B. Borland, 1956.159
P. *113*

Bedcover with Cigar- or Tobacco-Box Rectangles
Made by Theresa Zett Smith (American;
1866–1920)
New York, Syracuse; 1913
Borders: silk, satin weave; embroidered with
silk yarns in rosette chain stitches; pieced with
108 flags of cotton, twill weave; engraved roller
printed; fulled
226.7 × 181.3 cm (89¼ × 73⅜ in.)
The Textile Society of The Art Institute of
Chicago Dr. Lawrence S. Thurman Memorial
Fund, 1990.131
Pp. *114* (detail), *115*

TEXTILES FOR CHICAGO INTERIORS

Portière for James A. Patten House, Evanston, Illinois
Designed by George Maher (American; 1864–
1926) and Louis J. Millet (American; 1853–1923)
United States, 1901
Silk, wild silk, and cotton, plain weave, cut
solid velvet; appliquéd with silk and cotton,
satin damask weave; gilt-metal-strip-wrapped
linen and linen, satin weave; and cotton and
silk, plain weaves; embroidered with cotton,
linen, silk, and gilt-metal-strip-wrapped linen
in chain, cross, and overcast stitches
203.7 × 121.9 cm (80⅛ × 48 in.)
Restricted gift of the Antiquarian Society of The
Art Institute of Chicago, 1971.680
P. *116*

Carpet for Henry B. Babson House, Riverside, Illinois
Designed by George Grant Elmslie (American;
1871–1952)
United States, 1908/12

Linen, cotton, and wool, plain weave with
"Ghiordes knots" cut pile
560.1 × 115.7 cm (220½ × 45½ in.)
Restricted gift of Mrs. Theodore D. Tieken,
1972.1144
P. *117*

MODERN EUROPEAN YARDAGE

Panel Entitled "Poppyheads" (*Mohnköpfe*)
Designed by Koloman Moser (Austrian; 1868–
1918); woven and produced by Johan Backhausen & Söhne
Austria, Vienna; 1900
Silk, wild silk, and cotton, satin weave self-
patterned by ground weft floats
182.9 × 113 cm (72 × 44½ in.)
repeat: 45.5 × 29.8 cm (17⅞ × 11¾ in.)
Restricted gift of Mrs. Julian Armstrong, Jr.,
1986.963
Pp. *118–19*

Panel Entitled "Santa Sofia"
Designed by Josef Hoffmann (Austrian; 1870–
1956); printed and produced by the Wiener
Werkstätte
Austria, Vienna; 1910/12
Silk and cotton, plain weave; screen printed
135.7 × 114.6 cm (53⅜ × 45⅛ in.)
repeat: 37.4 × 24.1 cm (14¾ × 9½ in.)
Gift of Robert Allerton, 1924.217
P. *120*

Panel Entitled "The Harvest" (*La Moisson*)
Designed by Raoul Dufy (French; 1877–1953);
printed and produced by Bianchini Ferier
France, Lyon; 1920
Cotton and linen, plain weave; block printed
187.9 × 121.7 cm (74 × 47⅞ in.)
repeat: 74 × 38.6 cm (29⅛ × 15⅛ in.)
Purchase, 1924.611
P. *121*

Carpet
Designed by Jacobus W. G. (Jaap) Gidding
(Dutch; 1887–1955)
The Netherlands; 1920/25
Cotton, jute, and wool, plain weave with sec-
ondary binding warps tying chenille facing
wefts forming surface pile

297.6 × 196 cm (117¼ × 77⅛ in.)
Restricted gift of Mr. and Mrs. Robert Hixon
Glore in honor of Robert Hixon Glore, Jr.,
1986.990
Pp. *122–23*

Curtain Panel
Designed by Josef Hillerbrand (German;
1892–1981); woven and produced by the
Deutsche Werkstätten, AG
Germany, Munich; 1920/27
Cotton, machine-made lace: twist net; machine
embroidered laid work and couching
250.5 × 148.8 cm (98¾ × 58½ in.)
repeat: 17.8 × 15.5 cm (7 × 6⅛ in.)
Gift of Robert Allerton, 1927.795a
P. *129*

Panel
Designed by Elisabeth Raab (German; b. 1904);
printed and produced by the Deutsche
Werkstätten, AG
Germany, Munich; 1920/27
Linen, plain weave; block printed
205.4 × 127.2 cm (80⅞ × 50 in.)
repeat: 56.5 × 62.1 cm (22¼ × 24⅜ in.)
Gift of Robert Allerton, 1927.777
P. *128*

Border
Designed by Mariano Fortuny y Madrazo
(Spanish; 1871–1959); printed and produced
by the Società Anonima Fortuny
Italy, Venice; 1920/30
Cotton, twill weave; printed in the Fortuny
system
895.1 × 31.8 cm (352½ × 12½ in.)
repeat in warp direction: 146.2 cm (57½ in.)
Gift of Vera Megowan, 1981.99
Pp. *124–25*

Panel
Designed by Maria Monaci Gallenga (Italian;
1880–1940); printed and produced at Atelier
Gallenga
Italy, Rome; 1920/30
Cotton, plain weave, cut solid velvet; stencilled
317 × 132.3 cm (124¾ × 52 in.)
repeat: 78.8 × 32.4 cm (31 × 12¾ in.)
Gift of the Auxiliary Board of The Art Institute
of Chicago, 1990.223
P. *126*

Panel
Designed by Leon Bakst (Russian; 1866–
1924), 1922/23
France, 1923/24
Silk, twill weave; screen printed
141.1 × 96.9 cm (55½ × 38⅛ in.)
repeat: 26.4 × 51.2 cm (10⅜ × 20¼ in.)
Gift of Robert Allerton, 1924.184
P. *127*

MODERN AMERICAN YARDAGE

Panel Entitled "Boston"
Designed by Angelo Testa (American;
1921–1984)
Printed by Angelo Testa & Company
Illinois, Chicago; 1944
Cotton, plain weave; screen printed
91.7 × 123.6 cm (36 × 48⅝ in.)
repeat: 53.7 × 58.3 cm (21⅛ × 23 in.)
Gift of Angelo Testa and Alexander Demond
Fund, 1982.186
P. *132*

Panel from "The Taliesin Line"
After architectural designs by Frank Lloyd
Wright (American; 1867–1959); printed and
produced by F. Schumacher & Company
New York, New York; 1955
Rayon and silk, plain weave; screen printed
296.5 × 126.7 cm (116⅝ × 49⅞ in.)
repeat in warp direction: 67.7 cm (26⅝ in.)
Gift of Brooks Davis, 1983.176
Pp. *130–31*

Panel Entitled "Bamako"
Designed by Charles Edmund (Ed) Rossbach
(American; b. 1914) as prototype for custom-
designed yardage
California, Berkeley; 1960 (custom-produced
by Jack Lenor Larsen, Inc., New York, New
York, 1962/63)
Linen and silk, warp ikat dyed; plain weave
214.8 × 85.7 cm (84⅝ × 33⅝ in.)
repeat in weft direction: 57.2 cm (22¼ in.)
Gift of Ed Rossbach, 1985.750
P. *133*

THE TEXTILE AS ART OBJECT

Waters Above the Firmament
Designed and executed by Lenore Tawney
(American; b. 1907)
New York, New York; 1976
Linen, paper, and Liquitex, plain weave with
discontinuous wefts; braided, knotted, and cut
warp fringe; eighteenth/nineteenth-century

manuscript pages cut into strips, attached, and
painted with Liquitex
397.6 × 369 cm (156½ × 145¼ in.)
H. L. and Mary T. Adams, Harriott A. Fox, and
Mrs. Sigfried G. Schmidt endowments;
restricted gift of Laurance H. Armour, Jr.,
and Margot B. Armour Family Foundation,
Mrs. William B. Swartchild, Jr., Joan Rosenberg,
Joseph Fell, and the Textile Society of The Art
Institute of Chicago, 1983.203
Pp. *136* (detail), *137*

Morpheus
Designed and executed by Luba Krejci
(Czechoslavakian; b. 1925)
Czechoslovakia, Prague; 1979
Linen, lacis construction
203.1 × 222.2 cm (80 × 87½ in.)
Gift of Dr. and Mrs. Marshall D. Goldin,
1984.1556
P. *138*

Private Affair I
Designed by Claire Zeisler (American;
1903–1991); executed at Claire Zeisler Studio
Illinois, Chicago; 1986
Hemp, macramé (multiple chain knots),
twisted and wrapped cords; cut fringe
Approx. height 10½ feet and spill diam.
7½ feet as installed
Marion and Samuel Klasstorner Endowment,
1986.1050
P. *139*

**The Other Land
(*Das andere Land*)**
Designed by Lissy Funk (Swiss; b. 1909);
executed at Lissy Funk Studio
Switzerland, Zurich; 1986–87
Linen, plain weave; embroidered with linen,
wool, silk, horsehair, hemp, and gilt-metal-
strip-wrapped silk in open buttonhole filling
and stem stitches; laid work and couching
207 × 335 cm (81 12 × 131⅞ in.)
Restricted gift of the Women's Board of
The Art Institute of Chicago, Wirt D. Walker
Endowment, and Lissy Funk Acquisition Fund,
1989.414
Pp. *135* (detail), *140–41*

GLOSSARY

ANIMAL SUBSTRATE. A membranous animal substance (leather, parchment, or vellum).

APPLIQUÉING. A needlework technique for enhancing a foundation fabric by attaching to it pieces of another material, usually through stitching.

BLACKWORK. The name given to an English technique of thread-counted needlework on linen with black silk. The technique appeared during the reign of Henry VIII (1509–1547) and continued to be popular during Elizabethan times.

BLOCK PRINTING. A method of patterning the surface of a fabric with dye transferred through pressure from a carved wooden block.

BOBBIN LACE. Also known as pillow or bone lace. Lace made on a hand pillow to which has been attached a pattern drawn and pricked into parchment. The ends of lace threads, wound on bobbins (made of wood, bone, or ivory), are secured to the pillow and are plaited and twisted around pins that follow the pattern's outline. Bobbin laces can be straight-laces (made in one piece) or part-laces (made in separate motifs that are later joined).

BROCADING. A process of patterning a woven textile with a supplementary brocading weft while the piece is being woven. *See: Patterning and brocading wefts.*

BRUSSELS LACE. A term used to describe bobbin part-lace of a type initially produced in Brussels in the eighteenth century, distinguished by motifs worked with raised clothwork edges.

BUTTONHOLE STITCH. A simple looping stitch which is employed in needlework. It also is the foundation stitch of all needle lace.

CHINÉ. A technique of printing or resist dyeing warp threads prior to weaving. When warps are colored by printing, they are loosely woven with temporary wefts. After printing, the temporary wefts are removed, leaving a printed warp that is then rewoven into its final form.

COMPLEMENTARY WEFTS. More than one set of wefts that equally share in the formation of the ground weave. Complementary wefts exchange place and function within a weave to allow for color and pattern changes.

COPPER PLATE PRINTING. A method of patterning the surface of a fabric with dye transferred through the pressure of a press on an engraved copper plate.

COUCHING or **COUCHED STITCHES.** A needlework technique in which threads are laid over a pattern line or area and held in place by short stitches made through a foundation fabric. May be executed with a variety of stitches and patterns.

COVERLET. Derived from the Old French *covre lit*; refers to the function of the object — that of covering a bed.

CUT PILE / CUT VELVET / CUT AND VOIDED. *See: Velvet.*

CUT WORK. A needlework technique in which areas of a foundation fabric are cut away. The cut areas are finished with an embroidered stitch and/or filled with needle lace stitches. *See also: Drawn work.*

DAMASK WEAVE. A self-patterned weave of one warp and one weft set in which the pattern is produced by the juxtaposition of the warp and weft faces of the same weave.

DOUBLE CLOTH. A weave with two warp sets, each interlacing with its own weft set or sets, put on a loom so that two textiles are woven — in layers — simultaneously. These cloths can be completely separate from one another, joined by stitching ties, joined at the selvages, or joined through patterning achieved by exchanging the position of each set of warps on the loom while weaving.

DRAFT. The detailed, diagrammed instructions for placing patterns on a shaft loom.

DRAWN WORK. A needlework technique in which counted warp or weft threads are removed from a foundation fabric and the remaining threads are worked with decorative stitches. Also called *punto tirato*.

EMBROIDERING. Embellishing a foundation fabric with decorative stitches by using needle and thread.

ENGRAVED METAL ROLLER PRINTING. *See: Roller printing.*

FACING WEFTS. A supplementary weft set that passes from selvage to selvage and is bound on the face of a weave to enrich and/or provide textural contrast. Supplementary facing wefts are very often a metal strip or yarn.

FILLING STITCHES. (1) A single repeated stitch used to fill a pattern area of lace or other needlework with a texture. (2) A combination of embroidered stitches worked in repeated sequences to form a repeat pattern.

FLOAT(S). A warp or weft passing unbound over two or more elements of the opposite set.

FOUR-HARNESS LOOM. A loom equipped with four shafts, which raise and lower groups of warps in unison.

FULLED. A finishing process that gives a felted appearance to a woven cloth through the application of heat, moisture, and pressure.

FUSTIAN. A coarse fabric of cotton and linen.

GLAZED. A finishing process that gives a smooth and glossy appearance to a woven cloth through the application of heat, pressure, chemical action, or a glazing medium.

GOLD AND SILVER THREAD. *See: Metal thread.*

GROUND WEAVE. The basic interlacing system of warp and weft sets, which forms the structure or foundation of the finished textile.

IKAT DYED. A pattern resist dyed onto the warp, weft, or both warp and weft threads prior to weaving.

LACIS. A needlework technique of embroidering on a ground of knotted netting, or filet. Often executed in cloth or darning stitches, it produces a solid pattern on an open background.

LAID WORK. A needlework technique for filling large areas with closely laid long stitches attached to the ground fabric only at the ends of the area to be filled. These laid stitches are usually held in place within their span by couching stitches.

LOOPED STITCH. A stitch based on a crossed loop of yarn worked through a foundation fabric. Needle lace is based on interworked looping stitches.

MACRAMÉ. A needlework technique of building up a fabric from the knotting and plaiting of rows of vertical threads.

METAL THREAD. May be silvered or gold. May be of metal beaten into foil and cut into strips, metal wire, or a foil adhered to paper or an animal substrate.

NEEDLE LACE. General term that defines laces made with a needle and thread. Major motifs are outlined by tacking a heavy thread through a supported design on paper or parchment and the lace is constructed along these threads by executing interconnected, looped stitches.

NEEDLEWORK. General term that encompasses many techniques; employing a needle to embellish a foundation fabric with thread, such as appliqué, laid work, pulled thread, and cut and drawn work.

OPUS TEUTONICUM. *See: White work.*

OR NUÉ. A needlework technique that employs gold threads laid horizontally, generally on a plain woven linen foundation, held in place through tightly couched polychrome silk threads.

PATTERNING WARPS. A supplementary set of warps that patterns the ground weave.

PATTERNING AND BROCADING WEFTS. Supplementary weft sets, in addition to those forming the ground weave, which produce the pattern. Supplementary patterning wefts extend the full width of the fabric and are visible on the face of the weave only as required by the pattern. Supplementary brocading wefts are inserted only in those areas of the weave where patterning is required.

PICOTAGE. A term used to describe a dotted background in block printed textiles. Achieved by driving nails into the carved wooden block used to print the pattern.

PIECING or **PIECED QUILT.** Assembling and joining pieces of various fabrics into larger cloths, usually with a needle and thread. In pieced quilts, shaped pieces of fabric joined in this fashion are then quilted.

PILE. (1) A surface formed during weaving by supplementary elements that project from the foundation weave. (2) A surface embellishment of projecting threads formed through a needlework technique or a woven foundation.

PILE-ON-PILE VELVET. *See: Velvet.*

PLAIN WEAVE. The most basic weave, requiring two warp and weft groups in balanced alternation.

POINT DE GAZE. A mid-nineteenth century term for a Brussels needle lace characterized by motifs with raised outlines formed by bundles of threads loosely oversewn in buttonhole stitches, and spaces filled with elaborate buttonhole stitches. The light net ground is worked along the pattern edges and is powdered with tiny buttonhole rings.

PULLED THREAD WORK. A needlework technique in which embroidered elements divert threads of the foundation fabric out of their woven alignment by wrapping and tightly pulling sets of warps or wefts together and forming open areas in the foundation fabric.

QUILT. Bedcover formed by the process of quilting, that is, by stitching or sewing two layers of cloth together with a soft filling in between the layers. In the process, the stitching produces the pattern.

ROLLER PRINTING. A method of surface patterning a fabric with dye transferred to the fabric passed between a wooden cylinder carved or decorated with copper strips and pins, or by an engraved metal cylinder and a pressure roller.

RUNNING STITCH. The most basic stitch, which moves in a straight line, in and out of a fabric, creating floats on each side.

SATIN DAMASK WEAVE. A weave based on satin interlacing. *See: Damask weave.*

SATIN WEAVE. A simple float weave requiring a minimum of five warp and weft sets in which warps float over a minimum of four wefts, are never bound by more than one weft, and the diagonal alignment of floats is prevented by maintaining at least one intervening warp between binding points on successive wefts.

SCREEN PRINTING. A method of surface patterning a fabric by forcing a thick dye through a stretched screen onto which the negative of a design has been transferred. The pattern may be transferred by painting directly onto the screen, cutting and applying a stencil, or using photo-mechanical techniques. The dye paste is applied to the fabric by pushing it through the screen with a squeegee. One screen is required for each color.

SECONDARY BINDING WARPS. A secondary set of warps that does not participate in the formation of the ground weave. Secondary binding warps secure supplementary wefts or self-patterning weft elements to the ground weave and/or form a supplementary binding system with these elements.

SELF-PATTERNING GROUND WEFTS. Wefts belonging to the set that forms the ground or foundation weave, suspending its ground weave interlacing order so as to pattern the weave surface by floating unbound, or by interlacing with a secondary binding warp set in a supplementary interlacing order.

SELVAGES. The vertical, warp edges of a textile; the point at which the wefts turn on the warps.

SLIP DESIGN. A design drawn on fabric to be embroidered and/or appliquéd onto another surface.

SLIT TAPESTRY WEAVE. *See Tapestry weave.*

TAPESTRY. Properly used, this term applies only to large, tapestry-woven hangings.

TAPESTRY WEAVE. A simple weft-faced weave, woven in different colors of discontinuous wefts. These wefts do not travel from selvage to selvage but intersect only with warps in the areas where their color is needed. When areas of two colors meet along adjacent warps, an opening, or slit, is formed between those warps. Slits can be closed by using various tapestry-weave techniques:

Dovetailed Tapestry Weave, in which the wefts of two adjacent areas overlap on a common warp, eliminating the slits.

Interlocking Tapestry Weave, in which the wefts of two adjacent areas are linked together, between warps, thus eliminating the slits.

Slit Tapestry Weave, in which the wefts are not interwoven with each other at their edges, causing slits to appear between them.

TENT STITCH. A needlework stitch usually executed on an open, plain weave ground, known as canvas. It is worked in rows moving diagonally over one warp and weft intersection on the face and behind two warps and one weft on the reverse.

TIE-UP DIAGRAM. A diagrammed notation, part of a weaver's draft, which shows the connections required from the shafts to the treadles to produce a given weave on a shaft loom.

TWILL WEAVE. A simple float weave requiring a minimum of three warp and weft sets where warps are bound on successive wefts producing a diagonal alignment of binding points. This can be achieved through a variety of techniques:

Broken Twill Weave, in which the diagonal alignment is broken and the direction of the diagonal is reversed in every third weft passage without altering the interlacing order of the weave.

Chevron Twill Weave, in which the direction of the diagonal is reversed along an axis in the warp (warp chevron) or weft (weft chevron) direction. The effect is a zig-zag pattern, also known as herringbone.

Diamond Twill Weave, in which the direction of the diagonal is reversed in both the warp and weft directions. The resulting effect is that of a diamond shape.

UNCUT PILE. *See: Velvet.*

VELVET. A weave with a woven pile formed by supplementary pile warps, which are raised above the ground weave and over rods introduced during the weaving. The rods are removed after inserting several sheds of weft, which hold the supplementary pile warps in loops above the ground weave. Pile may be cut or uncut.

Cut Pile results when loops of pile warp are cut by inserting and pulling a knife through a groove in the rods.

Pile-on-Pile is a velvet weave with two or more levels of pile, formed during weaving by the use of two or more heights of rods. Pile-on-pile velvet may be either cut or uncut.

Solid Velvet describes velvet in which the ground weave is completely covered by pile.

Voided Velvet describes velvet in which areas of ground weave are visible, as supplementary pile warps are not raised above the ground weave to form pile. The areas of pile may be cut or uncut.

WARP(S). The vertical threads of a textile that are stretched on the loom before weaving.

WARP-FACED. A textile in which the warp is predominant and/or conceals the weft on the face of the weave.

WEAVING. The process of making a textile on a loom by interlacing warp and weft threads in a specific order.

WEFT(S). The horizontal threads of a textile that intersect the warp threads at right angles.

WEFT-RIBBED. A ribbed effect in the weft direction. Ribs are formed when the warp elements are numerically predominant and spaced so as to conceal the element.

WHITE WORK. A needlework technique in which all embroidered elements and the foundation fabric are white. Also called *Opus Teutonicum*, or German work.

WOODBLOCK. *See: Block printing.*